A Simplified Guide
to Worshiping As Lutherans

JAMES ALAN WADDELL

WIPF & STOCK · Eugene, Oregon

A Simplified Guide to Worshiping As Lutherans

Wipf & Stock
A Division of Wipf and Stock Publishers
199 W. 8th Ave., Suite 3
Eugene, OR 97401
www.wipfandstock.com

ISBN 13: 9781498252881

For my wife, Lisa

Contents

List of Figures

Preface

THIS LITTLE book is a simplified version of a much larger study published in December of 2005 titled *The Struggle to Reclaim the Liturgy in the Lutheran Church: Adiaphora in Historical, Theological and Practical Perspective* (Lewiston, NY: Mellen, 2005). In the larger book I presented in some detail a Lutheran theology of worship based on Scripture, the Lutheran Confessions, and numerous other historical documents by such figures as Martin Luther, Philip Melanchthon, and Martin Chemnitz.

In part my motivation for publishing the longer study was the climate that has developed in the church, a climate in which personal opinions, rather than the hard data of authoritative sources, are relied upon to shape our theology of worship. While we should respect one another's opinions, it is not personal opinions that should shape our theology of worship, but rather Scripture and the Lutheran Confessions. The struggles over worship that we face in the church today are the result of placing personal opinions before these authoritative sources. Both sides of today's worship debate are guilty in this regard.

These struggles are experienced not just among pastors and theologians, but as strongly if not more strongly among God's people in local congregations everywhere. The rift over worship is most keenly felt here, because this is where worship happens. This is where Christ meets his people in Word and

Sacrament. This is where the need to provide a resource for evaluating songs for worshiping in Lutheran congregations is now at its timeliest.

Building on this motivation to provide a theology of worship articulated in exclusively Lutheran terms, this smaller book is the result of many requests for a simplified version that could be used on a much broader scale. I offer *A Simplified Guide to Worshiping As Lutherans* as a resource for pastors, church leaders, church musicians, worship committees, and lay people looking for positive guidance for the inclusion of contemporary forms in the Lutheran congregation.

I should add just a brief note about some of the references in this book. Occasionally I will mention that "some have said," or "as some have said." I have not included documentation in footnotes here, since that documentation already exists in great detail in the longer study, *The Struggle to Reclaim the Liturgy in the Lutheran Church*, which is available through a local library (via inter-library loan if the library does not have it), or you can access it under the heading "WorshipConcord Resources" at the following URL address: http://worshipconcord.wordpress.com/.

You will also notice, especially in the early chapters, that I write in the first person. This is so for two reasons. This book is a revised version of an oral presentation of rewritten material taken from the longer book. First person references also reflect that I am writing about my own experience. This is just to alert the reader ahead of time to that particular aspect of this book.

Here I want to express my gratitude to several individuals—to Christian Amondson, Tina Owens, and Raydeen Cuffee of Wipf and Stock Publishers. They took the manuscript through the editorial process with patience and sensitivity, and made the publication process an enjoyable one.

Also with gratitude to my brother Brian Waddell for urging me to rewrite the longer study in a simpler form. I also want to thank Alan Sommer, Jeff Jordan, Tom Zelt, Bob Newton, Dale Sattgast, Chris Boehnke, and Toby Heller, all Lutheran pastors who read the longer study and invited me to speak at their district pastors conferences about the worship issues the church faces; they also encouraged me to develop it for a broader audience. Along with Chris Boehnke, Alan Sommer, and Tom Zelt, there is a group of lay people, pastors, teachers, and professors who share a positive vision for having a constructive conversation about worship in the Lutheran Church. This conversation is called WorshipConcord—Kent Burreson, Stewart Crown, Tom Dubensky, Tom Engler, Tim Frusti, Rich Hill, David Loy, Tim Maschke, Larry Rast, John Rathje, Mike Schmid, and Dien Taylor. I extend my thanks and respect to them for having the courage to engage this difficult conversation in a positive, forward-looking way.

Further thanks to Andy Brown, Kathy Frehrking Chelton, Rich Hill, Mary Kruta, and Chlo-Ann Rizzo for reading the whole manuscript and offering many helpful suggestions for simplifying the text. And with warm affection I express my indebtedness to Scott and Amy Rohrs for their selfless generosity and for reading the manuscript and offering suggestions for revisions that simplified the text.

Introduction

THERE ARE so many books on worship that one can scarcely hope to read all of them. So it would seem to be a fair question: "Why another book on worship?" This book is intended to be a simplified guide for Lutheran Christians who are asking the question: "What does it mean to worship as a Lutheran in the twenty first century?" We all know why this question is being asked. Whether a congregation uses "traditional" worship forms or "contemporary" worship forms, or both, most of us know what it is like at least to attempt to have an intelligent conversation about worship. And many of us know what it is like to have that conversation morph into disagreement and hard feelings.

The concept of "worship wars" is as old as the church. It is possible to read about differences over worship practices in some of the earliest writings of the church fathers. It is also an issue, in its more recent manifestations, that has dogged Lutheran Christians for nearly half a century. It is not just a theological issue debated in ivory towers of academia. It is a matter of the most practical concern among all of God's people, when they are gathered by the Holy Spirit to receive his gifts in the worship life of the local congregation.

The churches of the East and the West use worship traditions with histories that go back many centuries. Some of these traditions have remained by and large the same over the years. Some have changed.

When Martin Luther reformed the church's liturgy in 1523, he called it *Formula Missae* (the *Latin Mass*). In the years immediately preceding the Reformation the Medieval church worshiped in Latin. Now that in itself was not the biggest problem. Among the many problems Luther sought to address when he reformed the Medieval Mass were 1) the use of the Mass as a sacrifice, that is, man's work offered to appease an angry God, 2) the way the lay people viewed some ceremonies of the Medieval Mass as mindlessly repetitive and superstitious ritual, 3) receiving only the body of Christ in the Lord's Supper, and 4) the use of the Mass as a good work by which the worshiper merited God's favor (contrary to the biblical teaching of God's grace in justifying the sinner). There were many other abuses, but these were so obviously contrary to the Bible and endangered saving faith.

Luther composed his *Deutsche Messe* (the *German Mass*) in 1526 to teach the Gospel to the young and the inexperienced. The central principle Luther relied upon for reforming the church's liturgy was the biblical teaching of justification—that a person is put in a right relationship with God, is forgiven all sin, and is given the promise of eternal life, solely because of what Jesus did on the cross, purely as a gift of God's grace, without any part of it accomplished in any way by the worshiping individual. Justification is the central teaching of the Bible, and Luther relied on justification to reform the church's liturgy.

This little book in many ways is intended to be a reflection of Luther's *German Mass*. Here we will discuss some of the most important issues that are central to the so-called "worship wars," that leave so many of God's people confused and bewildered over the "traditional vs. contemporary" divide in the church today. We will also discuss what it means to worship as Lutheran Christians in a twenty-first century context.

I have not simply copied the outline of Luther's *German Mass*. Instead, I have employed Luther's rationale for reforming the Medieval Latin Mass and translating it into German. In other words, I have applied the basic principles Luther himself employed in his reformation of the church's liturgy, the most important being the biblical teaching of justification.

We live in a time when it seems as though a majority of pastors and congregations have made their own attempts to reform the church's worship—whether in an effort to adapt more contemporary forms of worship or in an effort to restore historic forms of worship in the Lutheran congregation. How do we know when these changes are good and when they are not good for worshiping as Lutherans? There are so many different opinions, and it seems the conversation has become so confusing, that a simplified guide to worshiping as Lutherans would be a useful tool for pastors, lay people, church musicians, church leaders, and worship committees. It is my hope that this book will provide such a tool, to help Lutheran Christians come together in peace and joy around the gifts God has given to his church—the Gospel and the sacraments. May Christ grant peace to his church.

1

A Pastor's Story

Fɪʀsᴛ, ᴛᴏ introduce this whole topic of *A Simplified Guide to Worshiping As Lutherans*, I want to say something about my own story and how this project came about. It originated out of my experience as a parish pastor leading worship in a local congregation.

I was baptized as an infant in the Lutheran Church, raised in the conservative Midwest, in small-town, rural Missouri; also in Nebraska, where my family have been members of the same Lutheran congregation for nearly forty years.

Throughout my life I have been a member of, or have served in some capacity, twelve Lutheran Church–Missouri Synod congregations, three of which I served as pastor. Most of these congregations used *The Lutheran Hymnal* (1941). A few of them used *Lutheran Worship* (1982). And in all three of the congregations I served as pastor, we chanted the liturgy; in one almost all the liturgy was chanted every Sunday; in the others we chanted parts of the liturgy.

During my seminary training in the 1980s we were taught to value the assumptions of a particular point of view on worship known as Liturgical Theology, even though we did not call it Liturgical Theology.[1] (I will say more about

---

1. Liturgical Theology is a school of thought, originating out of

these assumptions in chapters 4 and 5.) For now I will just make the following brief points.

Liturgical Theology holds a very high view of the church's liturgy. It values the liturgical traditions of the church passed down from generation to generation. And it promotes the exclusive use of those traditions.

Liturgical Theology takes as its primary source of worship the printed hymnal. Its primary instrument is the pipe organ. And its primary music is expressed in classical forms and traditional hymns. Some have even gone so far as to say that the Lutheran chorale is a mark of the true church.[2] Liturgical Theology is suspicious of all "contemporary" forms of worship. It questions anything that has arisen from Western popular culture, or anything that has not been tested by time.

Liturgical Theology holds a very high view of the sacraments—Baptism and the Lord's Supper. These sacraments are precious gifts from God, delivering for us sinners God's unmerited grace and unconditional promise of salvation in the forgiveness of sins through faith in Jesus Christ. Liturgical Theology rightly values the delivery of these gifts in the sacraments. For this Liturgical Theology should be praised.

But for me, during the early years of my theological study, there was a nagging uncertainty that went along with all the rejoicing in these treasures of the church. I could not

---

Eastern Orthodoxy and Roman Catholicism. It holds liturgy to be an authoritative standard above Scripture and all other theology in the church. It is a school of thought that many Lutheran scholars of liturgy today accept and attempt to adapt into their own "Lutheran" expressions of Liturgical Theology. See the concise definition in the Glossary.

2. There is clearly a difference between a chorale and a praise song. In a nutshell, a chorale is a classic hymn in a traditional form. A praise song has a simpler, less complicated melody in a more contemporary form.

quite put my finger on the source of the uncertainty, but it was always there. I trusted what my mentors taught me by day. And I read the writings of our faith late into the wee hours of every morning.

I read the Scriptures. I read the Lutheran Confessions in the *Book of Concord.* I studied the sources. And I internalized the theology I received from these precious documents. As I considered all the assumptions of Liturgical Theology, I found myself repeatedly coming back to Article VII of the *Augsburg Confession* and Article X of the *Formula of Concord.* Article VII is the church's great confession defining the church; Article VII defines the church on the basis of the Gospel and the sacraments, apart from humanly instituted ceremonies. *Formula of Concord* X is the church's confession of church ceremonies as *adiaphora.*[3]

I diagramed Article VII and drew connections between the German and the Latin versions, trying to reconcile the assumptions of Liturgical Theology with our confession of the church and her ceremonies. Liturgical Theology sounded appealing. And I was (and still am) fully committed to my unconditional subscription to the Lutheran Confessions.[4] I worked with all my might to fit the two together.

3. I will introduce to you already at this point the concept of *adiaphora*. In chapter 6 I will explain in more detail what *adiaphora* are according to the Lutheran Confessions. Here it is enough to know that the definition of *adiaphora* is "things that are neither commanded nor forbidden by God." The sixteenth-century reformers applied this term to liturgical ceremonies instituted by men. Also see the concise definition in the Glossary.

4. An unconditional subscription accepts without reservation that all the teachings of the Lutheran Confessions are in complete agreement with sacred Scripture.

But the nagging uncertainty persisted. As long as I studied the Scriptures and the Lutheran Confessions through the lens of Liturgical Theology, I was troubled by the thought that something was not quite right.

It was like trying to fit a square peg into a round hole. To make it fit, you must either change the shape of the peg or change the shape of the hole. But then you end up with something entirely different. On the one hand I had Scripture and the Lutheran Confessions. On the other hand I had Liturgical Theology. And I was not about to change Scripture or the Lutheran Confessions to fit my Liturgical Theology. Although, as it turns out, this is precisely what some in the church are doing today. (This is a criticism that cuts in both directions, because there are also those in the church today who misread Scripture and the Lutheran Confessions to defend their uncritical adoption of contemporary forms of worship; I will say more about this in chapter 4.)

When I was called to parish ministry I had neither the time nor the desire to worry about the contemporary worship issue. My first call was to a dual-parish in northeast Missouri, and of the hundred or so people who regularly worshiped only one asked for contemporary worship. So from a purely practical point of view it made no sense even to consider contemporary worship.

Then I accepted the divine call to serve a congregation in Michigan. Several of the leaders of the congregation asked for a contemporary worship service. As soon as I began my ministry there I found out why. The congregation had experienced a three-year pastoral vacancy, and leadership in worship suffered as a result. Hymns were selected that the congregation could not, or would not, sing. And the liturgy was so badly done, it was no wonder the people were asking for something different. So one of the first things I did as their pastor was focus on doing the liturgy well. But even then, the requests for contemporary worship continued.

I resisted their request for almost two years, during which time I tried reasoning with my flock. "The historic liturgy is the only form of worship that pleases God," I said.

"Well, pastor, how do you know?"

"All contemporary worship is based on false doctrine," I said.

"But, pastor, where does it say that in Scripture?"

"The hymns of our tradition are time-tested and time-honored by the church. This is not true of contemporary worship songs," I said.

"But, pastor, who says they have to be time-tested and time-honored?" And the conversation went on like that.

As a parish pastor I have always taken seriously the responsibility to teach the members of my congregation. So I scheduled a series of talks on worship. My goal was to offer my congregation the opportunity to study the sources together and to teach these searching souls that the historic liturgy was the only way for us to go. I honestly expected the request for contemporary worship to go away after this. My method for achieving this goal was to present to the members of my congregation passages from the Scriptures and the Lutheran Confessions which I thought supported Liturgical Theology. I was comfortably secure that all the assumptions of Liturgical Theology would win the day, and that the members of my parish would rejoice in the gift God had given to his church, the historic liturgy, and abandon their "whim" of wanting a contemporary service.

As I prepared to teach the flock entrusted to my care, I poured over Scripture and studied the Lutheran Confessions, Article XV of the *Augsburg Confession* on ceremonies, Article XXIV on the Mass, Articles VII & VIII of the *Apology of the Augsburg Confession* on the church. I found myself returning to Article VII of the *Augsburg Confession* on the church and *Formula of Concord* X on ceremonies. Many passages throughout the Lutheran Confessions echo what Article VII confesses about humanly instituted ceremonies, and they consistently hold these two points in distinction from each other—the pure Gospel and the sacraments on the one hand, and humanly instituted rites and ceremonies in liturgy on the other hand. This point will be revisited in more detail in chapter 3.

I studied the writings of Martin Luther, his *Latin Mass* of 1523 and his *German Mass* of 1526. I studied the early Luther and the later Luther, his *Lectures on Galatians* (1519, 1535), the *Babylonian Captivity of the Church* (1520), and Luther's *On Christian Freedom* (1520). I read Luther's *A Treatise on the New Testament* (1520), *The Misuse of the Mass* (1521), and his Invocavit Sermons of 1522. I studied Luther's *Against the Heavenly Prophets* (1525), his *Exhortation to the Livonians* (1525), his *Confession Concerning Christ's Supper* (1528), his *Exhortation to All Clergy Assembled at Augsburg* (1530), Luther's *Psalm Commentaries* (1530, 1535), personal letters, and literally dozens of other writings of the Reformer.

I studied Philip Melanchthon's writings, his *Loci Communes*, his *Commentary on Romans*, various personal correspondences, and other Latin texts from the *Corpus Reformatorum*.[5] Mostly I focused on Melanchthon's detailed

5. Philip Melanchthon was one of the key figures in the Sixteenth-

arguments in the *Apology of the Augsburg Confession*. There is an enormous amount of material there related to the Gospel, the sacraments, liturgy, and *adiaphora*.

I dug around in library archives for Latin works of Matthias Flacius, who insisted that *adiaphora* cease to be *adiaphora* in a case of controversy and confession.[6] This is a position that ultimately was written out of the Lutheran Confessions, but surprisingly is still held by some in the Lutheran Church today. This is an important point that I will discuss in more detail in chapters 6 and 7.

I studied Martin Chemnitz, his *Examination of the Council of Trent* (especially what he wrote about traditions), which is invaluable for this discussion.[7] I read Chemnitz's *Loci Theologici*, his *Enchiridion* on the office of the ministry, and the *Kirchenordnungen* (or church orders) of the Braunschweig–Wölfenbüttel Duchy, where Chemnitz served as superintendent of the churches between the years 1568 and 1578. I also studied Chemnitz's *Iudicium* on Adiaphora, and I

Century Reformation. He was a close colleague of Martin Luther's at the University of Witttenberg. In collaboration with Luther and their other colleagues, Melanchthon was responsible for penning most of the Lutheran Confessions in the *Book of Concord*.

6. Matthias Flacius was a Lutheran scholar who studied under Luther and Melanchthon in Wittenberg, but who eventually adopted a point of view in opposition to Luther's and Melanchthon's views of worship as *adiaphora*. For an explanation of the biblical concept of "confession" see chapter 7.

7. Martin Chemnitz was yet another key figure of the Sixteenth-Century Reformation. He is credited with advancing the Lutheran Reformation among the second generation of Lutherans after Martin Luther's death. This is why Chemnitz has been referred to as the "Second Martin."

compared dozens of other Lutheran church orders from the sixteenth century.

All of this study of the primary sources changed my point of view on the church's liturgy. It allowed me to see that the nagging uncertainty that plagued me for so long revolved around three considerable points—1) that in the writings of present-day Lutheran theologians there are subtle contradictions and revisionist readings of authoritative texts; 2) that in these writings a new Law is being made out of the Gospel; and 3) that the prevailing model of confession among some in the Lutheran Church today has developed into a practice of correcting an error by confessing the error's opposite.

This is my story. This is how this project came about, from my experience as a parish pastor, intending to teach the members of my flock to appreciate the treasures of the church in historic liturgical forms. What I found instead was that the treasure is much deeper and wider than I had originally anticipated.

SUMMARY POINTS

- In an effort to teach my congregation the blessings of historic liturgical forms, and the many theological problems with contemporary worship, we studied Scripture and the Lutheran Confessions together.

- Studying the authoritative sources of the Lutheran Church reveals that there are certain theological inconsistencies between the point of view on worship known as Liturgical Theology and the Lutheran Confessions.

- Attempts to adapt Liturgical Theology to a Lutheran perspective suffer from subtle contradictions and revisionist readings of authoritative texts.

- Attempts to adapt Liturgical Theology to a Lutheran perspective also suffer the result of making a new Law out of the Gospel.

- Attempts to adapt Liturgical Theology to a Lutheran perspective have also adopted a model of confession that seeks to correct an error by confessing (or promoting) the error's opposite.

- Virtually all of the observations above also may be said of those who uncritically adopt contemporary forms of worship in Lutheran congregations.

STUDY / DISCUSSION QUESTIONS

1. This is one pastor's story. Share your own story about your experience with worship. But first, read Ephesians 4:1–6, and make every effort to share your story with the utmost respect for the person who might disagree with your point of view. The climate today is one in which offense is easily taken, because too often the way in which we share our personal opinions is filled with emotion and does not demonstrate respect for the other point of view. So share your story, but choose your words carefully.

2. Have you ever had a conversation about worship with your pastor or anyone else? How did that conversation go? Did it go just as you would have liked? How would you prefer it had gone?

3. Share a time when your personal study of the Scriptures (or the Lutheran Confessions) changed your point of view on something. This should always be our attitude when we approach these texts. Why is this an important attitude to adopt? What happens when we do not have this attitude? As you read through this simplified guide to worshiping as Lutherans, be open to having your personal opinion shaped by the hard data of Scripture and the Lutheran Confessions.

2

The State of the Conversation about Worship Today

THE CONVERSATION about worship in the Lutheran Church has taken a bad turn. Battle lines have been drawn, and the warfare has been engaged for some time now. For the sake of the Gospel in the church, for the sake of the church's mission and her ministry, it is time for us to move beyond the worship wars. It is time for us to reconsider the ways that we think about worship, and the ways that we speak to each other about worship. This is the direction in which we need to go, for the sake of the church and for the sake of the Gospel in the church.

But before we can say where we need to go, to move ourselves beyond the worship wars, first we need to have a better understanding of where we are. What is the state of the conversation about worship today? A dose of rigorous self-reflection is healthy, and I dare say it is way overdue.

Where we are in our conversation, or I should say our non-conversation, about worship is contentious disagreement, polarization, and impasse. For some reason we seem not to be able to discuss this important issue with those with whom we disagree. The conversation has become so emotional, and so defensive, that even appeal to reason and love between brothers and sisters in Christ seems to fall on deaf ears.

So, let's talk about contentious disagreement. In the *Apology of the Augsburg Confession* Philip Melanchthon wrote the following: "Nothing can be said so carefully that it can escape misrepresentation." (*Apology* VII & VIII.2) And Martin Luther wrote in his book, *On the Freedom of a Christian*, that there are those "for whom nothing can be said so well that they will not spoil it by misunderstanding it."

There is contentious disagreement over what liturgy is, and where liturgy comes from. Does it come from God or does it come from the church? There is disagreement over the role of liturgy in the church. Is liturgy for the delivery of the Gospel? Is liturgy only for the teaching of those who are already members of the church? Or is it for outreach and evangelism? Do we even need liturgy in the church any more? There is not a consensus in the church when we attempt to answer these questions.

There is contentious disagreement over contemporary worship. How do we define it? Where does it come from? Is it even possible to have "contemporary" worship in the Lutheran congregation? Again, there is not a consensus in the church on these questions.

Along with contentious disagreement there is polarization, the state of being at opposite and extreme points of view. In the Lutheran Church some have adopted an "Anything-Goes" approach to worship. Others have adopted a "Liturgical-Repristination" approach to worship.

The "Anything-Goes" point of view on worship is characterized by the slogan, "Adiaphora, therefore freedom!" Whatever it takes to get people to hear the Gospel and join the church, that is what we will do. If it means dressing up as clowns, handing out balloons, shooting off fireworks in the sanctuary, running animals up and down the aisles, standing on my head, whatever it takes, that is what we will do, as long as it "saves souls."

The inconsistency of the "Anything-Goes" point of view is that, while claiming to promote the Gospel in the church, what is done in the name of the Gospel actually distracts people from hearing the Gospel. We must always remind ourselves that the ends do not justify the means. And in this case the unfortunate reality is that the actual result is not the intended result.

Repristination is a point of view that seeks to restore old things to present use. It is always striving for the "pristine" or purest form. The "Liturgical-Repristination" point of view insists that we may use only historic liturgical forms. It is characterized by slogans like, "*Leitourgia divina adiaphora non est*," a Latin phrase that means "The divine liturgy is not adiaphora." This point of view follows a model of confession that seeks to correct an error by confessing (or promoting) the error's opposite. The most obvious example I can give you is this: since the Liturgical-Repristination perspective views all contemporary forms of worship to be in error, Liturgical-Repristination seeks to correct this "error" by exclusively using and promoting the opposite of contemporary forms of worship, namely, historic liturgical forms.

One of the inconsistencies of Liturgical-Repristination is that, just like the Anything-Goes point of view, they add to the liturgies in our hymnals—only Liturgical-Repristination adds things that have long fallen out of use in the Lutheran Church. Whether it is incense, or special vestments, or exorcisms at Baptism, the reintroduction of these practices gives just as much the appearance of novelty for some in our church body as contemporary worship does for others.

Contentious disagreement and polarization between these two points of view have resulted in impasse. Webster defines impasse as "a predicament affording no obvious escape; a deadlock." On our theology and practice of worship in the Lutheran Church we are deadlocked in opposing, polarized views, unable and too often unwilling to have a meaningful conversation with each other.

The impasse has come to hardened perspectives. Each side is convinced of its own correctness. While both sides cannot be right, it is also a clear possibility that neither side is correct.

Hardened perspectives are no longer open to the persuasion of others. Convinced of my own correctness, and the error of the one with whom I disagree, why should I even bother to listen to what he has to say? So that's it. I'm right. You're wrong. End of discussion. This is where we are.

Shoving our collective head in the sand and ignoring each other may give us the immediate impression that we have avoided conflict, but in reality we only internalize our feelings, which (if not dealt with in a Christian manner) become more and more hardened with the passing of time. This is an approach that does not make the problem go away. In the end, polarized conflict over our theology and practice of worship remains, and eventually morphs into a dragon we would rather not slay.

In order to make some sense of the state of the conversation in the Lutheran Church today, it would be helpful to take a brief look at how it is we came to be in this prickly position on worship.

We all know about people who exhibit assertive aggressive and passive aggressive behaviors towards others. The assertive aggressive person gets in your face, points the finger (sometimes pokes it in your eye!), waves his arms in the air, ridicules those who disagree with him, and thinks he can shout others into submitting to his point of view. The passive aggressive person whispers in the corner, takes control of the conversation with a carefully massaged network of like-minded cronies, and stabs you in the back. Neither of the two is open to being reasoned with. These are the people who can make life together in the church absolutely miserable. Not only does this happen among lay people. It also happens among pastors and church leaders in the church's debate over worship.

Assertive aggressive behaviors in the conversation about worship run in the way of anger, raw sarcasm, ridicule, and name-calling. Assertive aggressive behaviors also run in the way of caricature and misrepresentation of differing points of view.

Let me illustrate this for you. If I bring a specific argument to the discussion, and someone else participating in the discussion dismantles my argument, this is certainly his prerogative, and it is a fair approach to debating any issue. I want the one with whom I disagree to be clear about every detail of my argument. But if that someone else, who has dismantled my argument, then takes the pieces of my argument and reconstructs them into an entirely different thing, and then demands that I defend the different thing as if *that* were my argument, this is an assertive aggressive caricature or a misrepresentation of my argument. It is intellectually dishonest and it happens all the time in the debate over worship. Unfortunately the intent is to defeat the person with whom there is disagreement, rather than being open to listening to what he has to say, and rather than being open to persuasion based on the hard data of Scripture and the Lutheran Confessions.[1] Let me give you two specific examples of how the conversation is skewed in this way.

Some who defend contemporary worship will paint the other side as if all historic liturgy is incense and high church, chasubles, miters, and "all the pomp of popery" as Luther called it.[2] Even the liturgies in our hymnals are treated like relics of a bygone era.

But this is flogging the straw man. It is a caricature of the countless thousands of congregations who use historic liturgical forms and are not "high church." The warning we are given in the Lutheran Confessions is that these things must not be made a matter of conscience, and we are free to use them or not use them as long as they do not cause offense and are not required as necessary acts of worship.

On the other hand, there are those who defend historic liturgical forms, and who argue in such a way that all contemporary worship is clown worship. They introduce their argument by describing the most extreme abuses of contemporary worship, and then advance their argument under the false pretense that all contemporary worship must be understood this way.

This also is caricature and misrepresentation, flogging the straw man. It is assertive aggressive, and it is intellectually

1. Being open to the persuasion of others (the Greek word is *epieikēs*, "reasonable, fair-minded") is one of the qualifications for the office of the ministry according to 1 Timothy 3:3. This should also be taken as an example for all Christians.

2. A chasuble is a liturgical vestment that an ordained pastor may wear over all his other vestments. It is traditionally worn for the celebration of the Lord's Supper. A miter is a tall pointed hat worn by bishops, cardinals, and popes.

dishonest. It happens over and over again in the non-conversation. I see this method of misrepresentation used article after article, in journals, in magazines, in blogs, and on websites. Of course we must remind ourselves that the Confessions warn us to avoid frivolity and offense in our worship practices. But we must also be honest about what is really going on.

In addition to assertive aggressive speech there are also passive aggressive behaviors in the conversation about worship. We ignore each other. We only have the conversation among those with whom we agree. And we refuse to talk to those with whom we disagree. This is unhealthy, and it does not please God.

With assertive and passive aggressive behaviors in the church comes conflict. Webster defines conflict in the following three ways: 1) to contend in warfare; 2) to show antagonism or irreconcilability; and 3) to have a collision. Now we typically view conflict as a negative thing. But we also should know that conflict can be both a negative and a positive experience.

There is both unhealthy and healthy conflict. The kinds of things that make conflict unhealthy are caricature and misrepresentation of the other's point of view, which thrives on misunderstanding and results in polarization and impasse. Healthy conflict on the other hand seeks conversation; it strives to understand the other's point of view, and it results in growth toward harmony.

The Apostle Paul wrote to the Philippians:

> If therefore there is any encouragement in Christ, if there is any consolation of love, if there is any fellowship of the Spirit, if any affection and compassion, make my joy complete by being of the same

> mind, maintaining the same love, united in spirit,
> intent on one purpose. Do nothing from selfish or
> empty conceit, but with humility of mind let each
> of you regard one another as more important than
> himself; do not merely look out for your own per-
> sonal interests, but also for the interests of others.
> (Philippians 2:1–4)

So far I have described two polarized points of view in the conversation about worship in the Lutheran Church. Struggling
against one another to the point of impasse, because we have
differing opinions over humanly instituted ceremonies is messy
business. Just to stay where we are, caricaturing each other, re-
fusing to listen to each other, and ignoring each other (as if the
problem will go away if we ignore it!), is not pleasing to God.

We need to move beyond this and ask the question, is
there a middle ground in this debate? If we claim that all traditional worship is high church, we do not make such a claim
from the middle ground. And if we claim that there can be
no contemporary worship forms in Lutheran congregations,
we do not make this claim from the middle ground, even if
we think we do. So where is the middle ground in the debate?
How do we define it?

I am not talking about sitting on the theological fence,
or being non-committal about liturgy. What I am talking
about is a clear definition and confession of the biblical and
confessional point of view on the church's liturgy. Is there a
middle ground?

How do we define the "middle ground"? Those who
hold to the middle ground in this discussion have not been
privileged to have their voices heard. They have been silenced.
They have been ignored. They have been ridiculed. And they

are frustrated. I know. I am a pastor who speaks from that middle ground. How far can we go and still be faithful to our Lutheran Christian identity?

The intent here is to give a voice to the middle ground, to facilitate the conversation about worship between brothers and sisters in Christ in Lutheran congregations troubled by the worship wars. Hopefully the conversation initiated by this book will foster another conversation, and another, and another, until we all attain unity in the faith (with respect to worship) and knowledge of the Son of God, making every effort to maintain the unity of the Spirit through the bond of peace, as the holy Apostle wrote in his Letter to the Ephesians (4:1–6).

SUMMARY POINTS

- Contentious disagreement, polarization, impasse, and hardened perspectives over worship forms characterize the state of the conversation about worship in the church today.

- The polarization over worship among Lutherans today may be described as "Anything Goes" vs. "Liturgical Repristination."

- Assertive aggressive approaches—anger, raw sarcasm, caricature, and misrepresentation of the other's point of view—do not contribute to a solution and only exacerbate the problem.

- Passive aggressive approaches to the problem—ignoring each other, only having the conversation with those with whom we agree, and ignoring the problem with the expectation that it will eventually go away all by itself—likewise do not contribute to a solution and further exacerbate the problem.

- One solution to the problem is to define and give voice to the middle ground in the debate according to Scripture and the Lutheran Confessions, following faith and clear reason.

STUDY / DISCUSSION QUESTIONS

1. How have you found the state of the conversation about worship in your own context? Whether you answered this question positively or negatively, why do you think it is this way?

2. Looking at the "bigger picture" in the Lutheran Church, what can we do to improve the state of the conversation about worship? What can you personally do to make this happen? Or should we just give in to our cynical nature (Old Adam), and concede that nothing can or should be done? Why or why not?

3. Why, do you suppose, is it so hard to have a "reasonable" conversation with someone who disagrees with you about worship? What might be a solution to this challenging problem? (Hint: the meaning of the Greek word, *epieikēs*, in 1 Timothy 3:3.)

4. Reflecting on the material in this chapter, how would you define the middle ground in the debate over worship? Be prepared to support your answer with clear reasons, and not just feelings. Why do you define the middle ground the way you do?

3

What Is Worship?

"WE VISITED the Lutheran church on the other side of town last Sunday. I didn't recognize anything in the service." Has this ever happened to you? How about this: "I can't relate to the music we sang in that church's service. It seems so outdated."

In one sense, these are real concerns expressed by Lutheran Christians who faithfully attend worship every week. The intent here is not to oversimplify, but there are essentially these two concerns. When a Lutheran Christian has grown up nurtured by what I will call hymnal liturgy, anything else seems odd, unusual, foreign.[1] When a Lutheran Christian has not grown up nurtured in this same way, then it is the hymnal liturgy itself that seems odd, unusual, foreign. Both of these are real, equally legitimate concerns expressed by God's people in the church. Neither of these concerns should be simply dismissed. On the other hand, according to the Lutheran point of view, these are not the most important things.

---

1. My use of the term "hymnal liturgy" is not derogatory and is in no way to imply that the hymnal is not to be valued. On the contrary, the historic liturgical forms of the hymnal are a great treasure of the church.

THE MOST IMPORTANT THINGS

Regarding worship, what matters most according to the Lutheran point of view are the Gospel preached in its truth and purity and the sacraments given according to Scripture. The Apostle Paul put it this way when he wrote to the Christians of Corinth, emphasizing the primary importance of the Gospel:

> Now I would remind you, brothers, of the gospel I preached to you, which you received, in which you stand, and by which you are being saved, if you hold fast to the word I preached to you—unless you believed in vain. For I delivered to you as of first importance what I also received: that Christ died for our sins in accordance with the Scriptures, that he was buried, that he was raised on the third day in accordance with the Scriptures . . . . (1 Corinthians 15:1–4)

According to the Apostle Paul, what is "of first importance" is the Gospel he had received from the risen Christ. Paul articulated this Gospel in the simplest of terms "in accordance with the Scriptures"—the death, burial, and resurrection of Christ for us and for our salvation.

The Apostle also wrote to the Corinthians with reference to the sacraments (here referred to as "mysteries"): "This is how one should regard us, as servants of Christ and stewards of the mysteries of God." (1 Corinthians 4:1) Stewards are given to make use of things that do not belong to them, to use these things in the way that the Owner has given them to be used. In another place in 1 Corinthians, Paul makes it clear that Christ is the Owner, or Giver, of the Sacrament:

> For I received from the Lord what I also delivered
> to you, that the Lord Jesus on the night when he
> was betrayed took bread, and when he had given
> thanks, he broke it, and said, "This is my body
> which is for you. Do this in remembrance of me."
> In the same way also he took the cup, after supper,
> saying, "This cup is the new covenant in my blood.
> Do this, as often as you drink it, in remembrance of
> me." For as often as you eat this bread and drink the
> cup, you proclaim the Lord's death until he comes.
> (1 Corinthians 11:23–26)

The One who gives the gift desires that his gift be used in the way that he gives it. Anything else and it becomes something other than what he has given. This is why Paul wrote to the Corinthians that they had so abused their use of the Sacrament that it was "not the Lord's Supper that you eat." (1 Corinthians 11:20) This is also why the Apostle repeats verbatim the words of the Lord just as he received them from the Lord—"For I received from the Lord what I also delivered to you . . . ." This is what the steward of God's mysteries is called to do, to give the gifts of God to the people of God as God himself has given them. These two things (the Gospel and the sacraments), and these only, are what matter most according to Scripture, and the Lutheran point of view always strives to be faithful here.

In the sixteenth century the reformers defined the church in precisely these terms. Article VII of the *Augsburg Confession* puts it this way:

> It is also taught among us that one holy Christian
> church will be and remain forever. This is the as-
> sembly of all believers among whom the Gospel

> is preached in its purity and the holy sacraments are administered according to the Gospel. For it is sufficient for the true unity of the Christian church that the Gospel be preached in conformity with a pure understanding of it and that the sacraments be administered in accordance with the divine Word. It is not necessary for the true unity of the Christian church that the ceremonies, instituted by men, should be observed uniformly in all places. It is as Paul says in Eph. 4:4–5, "There is one body and one Spirit, just as you were called to the one hope that belongs to your call, one Lord, one faith, one baptism." (*Augsburg Confession* VII)

So we have these two aspects of our worship taking place at the same time—the preaching of the Gospel and the giving of the sacraments (Baptism and the Lord's Supper) on the one hand, and ceremonies instituted by men on the other hand. The only part of this that is necessary for the true identity of the Christian church, however, is the purity of the Gospel and the sacraments given in accordance with the Word of God. What is not necessary for the true identity of the church is uniformity of ceremonies that have been instituted by men. According to Scripture and the Lutheran Confessions we may say that the church is defined sacramentally according to the Gospel.

What is the purity of the Gospel? The Gospel is this and only this, that our merciful God gave his Son to be born as a human being, to be crucified on a cross to pay the penalty for our sin. The Gospel is that Jesus suffered, shed his blood for us, and died on the cross, to redeem us lost and condemned creatures, and that in the flesh he rose alive from the grave on the third day to give us the promise and hope of the resurrection to eternal life.

We all know the passage from the New Testament where John (3:16–17) records that Jesus had a conversation with Nicodemus. Jesus told this searching Pharisee: "For God so loved the world, that he gave his only Son, that whoever believes in him should not perish but have eternal life. For God did not send his Son into the world to condemn the world, but in order that the world might be saved through him." This is the Gospel: God loves us, and it is because he loves us that he gives himself to us. When it comes to the Gospel, God is the one who does what needs to be done. And he does it for us, for our salvation.

The Gospel is not me adding anything to what God did for us in Jesus Christ. The Gospel does not include me "accepting" what God did for us in Jesus Christ. The Gospel does not include me "adoring" God for what he did for us in Jesus Christ. And it does not include me "announcing" that "God alone is worthy of my praise" for what he did for us in Jesus Christ. The Gospel includes none of this. If anything, this is our response of faith to the Gospel. But it is not itself the Gospel.

The Gospel is this and only this, that "in Christ God was reconciling the world to himself, not counting their trespasses against them" (2 Corinthians 5:19), period. The Apostle Paul put it this way in his Letter to the Ephesians (2:1–10):

> And you were dead in the trespasses and sins in which you once walked, following the course of this world, following the prince of the power of the air, the spirit that is now at work in the sons of disobedience—among whom we all once lived in the passions of our flesh, carrying out the desires of the body and the mind, and were by nature children of

> wrath, like the rest of mankind. But God, being rich in mercy, because of the great love with which he loved us, even when we were dead in our trespasses, made us alive together with Christ—by grace you have been saved—and raised us up with him and seated us with him in the heavenly places in Christ Jesus, so that in the coming ages he might show the immeasurable riches of his grace in kindness toward us in Christ Jesus. For by grace you have been saved through faith. And this is not your own doing; it is the gift of God, not a result of works, so that no one may boast. For we are his workmanship, created in Christ Jesus for good works, which God prepared beforehand, that we should walk in them.

". . . even when we were dead . . . ." The Apostle refers to being "dead" twice. Do you see? A corpse cannot resuscitate itself. Not only is it true that we *do not* contribute to our salvation by participating in the Gospel. But God's Spirit through the holy Scriptures makes it absolutely clear that we *cannot* contribute to our salvation by our participation in the Gospel. The Lord told his disciples: "You did not choose me, but I chose you." (John 15:16) This is why Paul refers to salvation as God's work of grace, and not in any way our work of fulfilling any requirement of the Law. The Apostle Paul wrote to the Romans: "But if it is by grace, it is no longer on the basis of works; otherwise grace would no longer be grace." (Romans 11:6)

There is nothing, in any way, shape, or form, that this once dead, sinful bag of worms can add to what God did for us in Jesus Christ. The Prophet Isaiah's statement, ". . . all our righteous deeds are like a polluted garment" (Isaiah 64:6), is a graphic illustration of this. There is not one thing in, with, or by my person—whether thoughts, words, or deeds—that I can use even to insinuate a contribution to my salvation. I am only an unworthy recipient of this gift, this precious, costly, priceless treasure of the new life God gives me in his dearly loved Son. This is the purity of the Gospel.

What does it mean that the sacraments are to be given in accordance with God's Word? Is this an implied reference to "the liturgy that the Lutheran Confessions *assume*," as some have said? Or they refer to "the meaning and the intention of the Lutheran Confessions' comments about worship," with the preconceived conclusion that the Confessions are referring to a specific liturgical form. Here I would simply ask of those who say this, which liturgy is that? Would it be Luther's *Latin Mass* (1523) or Luther's *German Mass* (1526)? They are both very different, and they were both in existence already before the *Augsburg Confession* (1530) was composed.

So we need to be clear; when *Augsburg Confession* Article VII states that the sacraments are to be given in accordance with God's Word, does this refer to historic traditional forms of the church's liturgy? Some have indeed said this (and continue to say this). What does this mean? If this is not an implied reference to "the liturgy that the Lutheran Confessions *assume*," then what does it refer to?

The entire context of the *Book of Concord* (which includes all the Lutheran Confessions), along with several historic documents leading up to the composition of the *Augsburg Confession*, are most helpful here.[2] These documents demonstrate precisely what the reformers meant when they referred to the sacraments being given in accordance

2. For access to these documents in English see *Sources and Contexts of the Book of Concord*, Robert Kolb and James A. Nestingen, eds. (Minneapolis: Fortress, 2001).

with God's Word. That is, they show how the reformers confessed that Baptism is God's work of grace, and how Baptism cleanses the person from sin and gives the promise of eternal life, as opposed to the understanding that Baptism is a work that we do or that Baptism is evidence that we have "asked Jesus into our hearts."

These documents also show how the reformers confessed that in the Lord's Supper the true body and blood of Christ are given for the forgiveness of sins; that it is not just symbolic, but is true presence of Christ's body and blood. There is no reference in any of these texts that makes a connection between sacraments given in accordance with God's Word on the one hand, and humanly instituted ceremonies in liturgy on the other hand. So the phrase in *Augsburg Confession* VII, "sacraments . . . administered in accordance with the divine Word," does not refer to humanly instituted ceremonies in liturgy, and it does not refer to any liturgy that the Lutheran Confessions "assume."

In order further to clarify the relationship between sacraments and ceremonies in liturgy, it would be helpful to see just how the Lutheran Confessions define liturgy.

LITURGY IN THE NARROW SENSE AND LITURGY IN THE BROAD SENSE

In ancient times one of the terms used for worship was *leitourgia*. This is where the word "liturgy" comes from. In the Greco-Roman world *leitourgia* referred to a public service rendered by an individual on behalf of the community (infrastructure, roads, bridges, public buildings), a city official giving himself for a period of service to do the administrative work of the Greek *polis*, or the taxes levied on individuals to support public facilities for the common good. In the Septuagint *leitourgia* referred to the entire system of worship in the Jerusalem temple.[3]

Let's look at what the *Apology of the Augsburg Confession* teaches about *leitourgia*. In the sixteenth century the Roman Catholic Church defined the Mass liturgy as a sacrifice. In other words, they viewed worship as something the priest did on behalf of the worshiping community, in order to appease God's wrath against human sin. In the *Apology's* Article XXIV on the Mass, by pointing out what *leitourgia* meant in the classical Greco-Roman world, Philip Melanchthon was able to clarify that the term *leitourgia* could not be used to defend the Roman Catholic error of the Mass as a sacrifice. The *Apology* reads:

> This word does not properly mean a sacrifice but rather public service. Thus, it agrees quite well with our position, namely, that the one minister who consecrates gives the body and blood of the Lord to the rest of the people, just as a minister who preaches sets forth the gospel to the people, as Paul says [in 1 Cor. 4:1], 'Think of us in this way, as servants of Christ and stewards of God's mysteries,' that is, of the gospel and the sacraments. (*Apology* XXIV.80)

The definition of "liturgy" in the *Apology* is consistent with the *Augsburg Confession's* definition of the church. As we have already seen, *Augsburg Confession* VII defines the church as "the assembly of all believers among whom the Gospel is preached in its purity and the holy sacraments are admin-

3. The Septuagint is the ancient Greek translation of the Old Testament.

istered according to the Gospel." This is how the Lutheran Confessions define "liturgy" or Christian worship, the preaching of the Gospel and the giving of the sacraments to the people. The Confessions clearly distinguish between this use of the term liturgy as the Gospel and the sacraments on the one hand, and the broader use of the term liturgy which refers to ceremonies instituted by men on the other hand. Not to make this distinction creates confusion.

There is both a narrow meaning of the term liturgy and a broad meaning of the term liturgy. **(See Figure-1)** The Lutheran Confessions use the term liturgy in the narrow sense. The broad meaning of the term liturgy, however, is what is most commonly used today.

Figure-1: The Narrow and Broad Senses of Liturgy

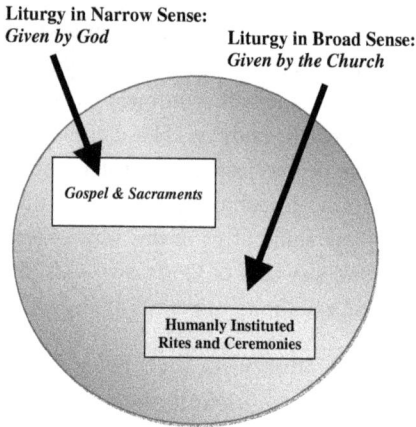

The narrow meaning of the term liturgy in the Lutheran Confessions simply refers to the Gospel and the sacraments. This is liturgy that belongs to God and that is given by God to the church. This is liturgy that should be received as it has been given by God, without change, liturgy in the narrow sense.

The broad meaning of the term liturgy, as it is most commonly used today, refers to all of it together, the preaching of the Gospel, the giving of the sacraments to the people, and all the rites and ceremonies instituted by men, as *Augsburg Confession* VII refers to them. This is liturgy in the broad sense, everything from the Trinitarian invocation to the benediction.

The failure to make this distinction between liturgy in the narrow sense and liturgy in the broad sense is, no doubt, one source of so much confusion over worship today. By not separating liturgy in the narrow sense from liturgy in the broad sense, this leads some to make the claim that liturgy in the broad sense is also given by God and that this liturgy should never be changed. But this is simply not the case.

Some today speak of a liturgy that is given by the Lord or a liturgy that belongs to the Lord. If we speak of liturgy in such a way, then this is true only if we are referring to what has been given by the Lord in the Gospel and the sacraments, liturgy in the narrow sense. Then the admonition is also true that we must not be changing what belongs to and what is given by the Lord—the Gospel preached in its purity and the sacraments given according to the Gospel. Only liturgy in this sense is liturgy that belongs to God and liturgy that is given by God. It is not ours to change this. It is ours to be stewards of what God has given.

Liturgy in the broad sense is what is given by the church and what belongs to the church. Liturgy in the broad sense is not given by God. And the argument that we must not be changing liturgy in the broad sense must be revisited.

The distinction between what is given by God (liturgy in the narrow sense) and what is given by the church (liturgy in the broad sense) is a distinction that is made in the Lutheran Confessions. This is a confessional concept that should shape our Lutheran theology of worship. According to the church's confession, the church is not defined liturgically in the broad sense, as has been said by some. According to the church's confession the church is defined liturgically only in the narrow sense, that is, it is defined sacramentally according to the Gospel.

Another word that was used for worship in the Lutheran Confessions is *cultus*. The reformers used this word, *cultus*, to refer to both the preaching of the Gospel and the human act of worship as a response of faith to the Gospel. In other words, sometimes they used the word *cultus* to refer to liturgy in the narrow sense, the preaching of the Gospel. But sometimes they used the word *cultus* to refer to liturgy in the broad sense, in contrast to the word *leitourgia*, which they used to refer to liturgy only in the narrow sense. This latter use of the word *cultus* in the Lutheran Confessions simply referred to the human act of worship as response of faith. At that time it did not have the specialized sense that it has today, when we use it to refer to a religious cult.

Two passages from the *Apology of the Augsburg Confession* will illustrate how the reformers used the word *cultus*. *Apology* XV.42 states that "the chief worship of God (*cultus Dei*) is to preach the gospel." With regard to worship, the Gospel should be at the center of everything, ". . . of first importance," as the Apostle Paul wrote. This use of *cultus* corresponds to liturgy in the narrow sense.

The second example is taken from *Apology* IV.154, where we have a description of worship as our reception of forgiveness from God. Here Melanchthon describes the experience of the woman who wet Jesus' feet with her tears and wiped them with her hair:

> The woman came, believing that she should seek the forgiveness of sins from Christ. This is the highest way of worshiping Christ.[4] Nothing greater could she ascribe to him. By looking for the forgiveness of sins from him, she truly acknowledged him as the Messiah. Truly to believe means to think of Christ in this way, and in this way to worship[5] and take hold of him. . . . [Christ] points to the woman and praises her reverence,[6] her anointing and crying, all of which were a sign and confession of faith that she was looking for the forgiveness of sins from Christ.[7]

This is what the reformers referred to as *cultus*, liturgy in the broad sense, the human act of worship as response of faith to God's unconditional love for us, his forgiveness, in Jesus Christ.

There is yet a third term the reformers used when they referred to the worship of God's people. That term is *Gottesdienst*. Literally translated *Gottesdienst* means "the service of God." The reformers used this word in three different

4. The Latin wording here is *Hic cultus est summus cultus Christi*.

5. Here the Latin word is *colere*, which is a form of the Latin word *cultus*.

6. Here we have *cultum*, yet another form of the Latin word *cultus*.

7. The account cited in this passage is located at Luke 7:36–50; see also Matthew 26:6–13; Mark 14:1–11; John 12:1–8.

ways. They used *Gottesdienst* to refer simply to liturgy in the narrow sense, that is, the purity of the Gospel and the sacraments administered in accordance with God's Word. They also used *Gottesdienst* to refer only to ceremonies in liturgy instituted by men, in contrast to the Gospel and the sacraments. And finally, they used *Gottesdienst* to refer to all of it at the same time, the Gospel and the sacraments together with all the humanly instituted ceremonies in liturgy. Each use of the word *Gottesdienst* in the Lutheran Confessions must be carefully understood in its own context, without confusing the uses or misconstruing the meanings. Misconstruing *Gottesdienst*, to mean only all the liturgy together as having been given by God (both in the narrow *and* the broad sense), has also contributed to much of the confusion in the conversation about worship today.

According to the Lutheran point of view on worship (based on Scripture and the Lutheran Confessions) the most important things are the Gospel in its truth and purity and the sacraments given in accordance with God's Word. The Lutheran point of view on worship (again based on Scripture and the Lutheran Confessions) also has this twofold understanding of worship: liturgy in the narrow sense and liturgy in the broad sense. One is given by God (liturgy in the narrow sense). One is given not by God, but by the church (liturgy in the broad sense). One must never be changed (Gospel and sacraments). One may be changed (humanly instituted ceremonies).

To say that these things *may* be changed is not to say that they necessarily *should* be changed. Neither is it a reasonable position to insist that everyone must change from historic liturgical forms to contemporary forms, in order for the church to grow. We will discuss this in more detail in chapter 7.

SUMMARY POINTS

- According to Scripture and the Lutheran Confessions, the most important things in worship are the purity of the Gospel and the sacraments given in accordance with God's Word.

- According to the Lutheran Confessions liturgy in the narrow sense is the purity of the Gospel and the sacraments given in accordance with God's Word.

- Liturgy in the narrow sense is given by God; this is the part of liturgy that should not be changed.

- Liturgy in the broad sense is all the ceremonies instituted by men added to the Gospel and the sacraments.

- Liturgy in the broad sense is given by the church; this is the part of liturgy that may be changed.

STUDY / DISCUSSION QUESTIONS

1. According to the Lutheran point of view, what are the most important things in worship? Where in the Bible does this view come from?

2. What is the purity of the Gospel? How do we sometimes get this wrong? Why is it important that we get this right?

3. What does it mean that the sacraments are to be given in accordance with God's Word? Why does this matter?

4. In the Greco-Roman world, what did the term *leitourgia* refer to? How does *Apology of the Augsburg Confession* XXIV.80 define *leitourgia*? How does this relate to *Augsburg Confession* Article VII?

5. What is liturgy in the narrow sense? What is liturgy in the broad sense? Why is it important to keep this distinction clear for a correct understanding of worship according to the Lutheran point of view? What happens when we fail to make this distinction?

4

Lutheran Assumptions about Worship

A N ASSUMPTION is something we often take for granted to be true, without bothering to investigate whether it actually is true. For example, pastors often hear their confirmation students say, "I'm not good at memorizing, so I won't do very well if you expect me to memorize." The assumption is, "I'm not good at memorizing." The (in this case negative) consequence of the assumption is that the student refuses to make the effort to memorize, resulting in limited learning. The assumption is shown to be false, however, when the student shows up for class singing a favorite song . . . that he's memorized(!). How did the student memorize his favorite song? By repetition; he listened to it over and over again (probably until his parents couldn't take it any more!).

Assumptions have consequences. In other words, the way in which we approach virtually everything determines ahead of time the conclusions we draw, the decisions we make, and the actions that follow. Assumptions are very powerful things. Unfortunately, too often we do not take the time (or make the effort) to examine the assumptions that drive our thinking and our actions.

Socrates put it this way: "An unexamined life is not worth living." A bit extreme, but there is a basic truth here nonetheless. And of course the Bible has something to say about the person who fails to reflect on his life in relation to God: "For if anyone is a hearer of the word and not a doer, he is like a man who looks intently at his natural face in a mirror. For he looks at himself and goes away and at once forgets what he was like." (James 1:23–24)

We all have assumptions that shape the ways we think and talk about worship. The real question is, are we willing to do the necessary critical self-reflecting? In other words, are we open to looking critically at our assumptions in light of Scripture and the Lutheran Confessions? This is really an indispensable aspect of the Christian life. The Apostle Paul wrote to the Corinthians: "Examine yourselves, to see whether you are in the faith. Test yourselves." (2 Corinthians 13:5)

We should always be up front about our assumptions. It does no one any good when we conceal our assumptions or when we are less than honest about where our assumptions come from, or even when we are unwilling to engage in (or are lazy about) critical self-reflection. In fact, everyone loses when we adopt this point of view. Likewise our methodology. If we begin with questionable assumptions and combine this with bad methodology, then we are going to end up in a wrong place on worship.

So, traditional or contemporary? What is our theological basis for making this choice? At some point all of us have had to choose between contemporary and traditional forms of worship, or whether to include contemporary forms of worship alongside traditional forms, or whether simply to ignore the issue altogether. The question is: What is our basis for making this choice? It would be helpful to begin by defining our terms.

I have already shown you how we get it wrong when we define traditional and contemporary worship. We do not define traditional worship only in terms of high church practices. And we do not define contemporary worship only as clown worship. We have seen how these are intellectually dishonest approaches to the problem.

In general, we may define all worship, both traditional and contemporary, the way Luther put it in his *Latin Mass* in 1523: "... the Scriptures prescribe nothing in these matters, but allow freedom for the Spirit to act according to his own understanding as the respective place, time, and persons may require it."

THE MOST IMPORTANT ASSUMPTIONS ABOUT WORSHIP

There are so many assumptions about worship, but I want to begin by laying out for you those that are distinctly Lutheran. Our assumptions about worship should be founded on the clear and simple principle: Lutheran theology for Lutheran worship. So what are Lutheran assumptions about worship? Many of these may already be familiar to you. There are two primary assumptions.

The first assumption is that justification by grace alone through faith alone for Christ's sake is the central biblical teaching of the Christian faith. There are two minor assumptions that go along with this. The first minor assumption is that the delivery of justification is central to the church's theology and practice of worship. The second minor assumption is that liturgical ceremonies instituted by men are not the main consideration; the Gospel and the sacraments are.

The second primary assumption is that liturgical ceremonies instituted by men are *adiaphora*, that is, things that are neither commanded nor forbidden by God. Keep in mind, however, that the Gospel and the sacraments themselves are not *adiaphora*, because they are not instituted by men; they are given by God (liturgy in the narrow sense). That liturgy in the broad sense is *adiaphora* does not mean, however, that anything goes, as we will see in what follows. All of these assumptions are based on what Scripture and the Lutheran Confessions teach us about the church's worship. They are founded on the clear and simple principle: Lutheran theology for Lutheran worship.

SOME OF THE MORE COMMON ASSUMPTIONS ABOUT WORSHIP

Since our assumptions, rather than Scripture and the Lutheran Confessions, have a way of running the debate, let's look at some of the more common assumptions about traditional and contemporary forms that contribute to misunderstanding and conflict when it comes to worship.

On the traditional end we assume that all contemporary forms of worship are bad for the church. We assume that change in worship has taken place only gradually over long periods of time. We assume that uniformity of liturgy is necessary for the unity of the church. And we assume that freedom in the use of *adiaphora* is always license. It is quite telling that none of these assumptions can be demonstrated from Scripture or the Lutheran Confessions.

On the contemporary end we assume that outreach is the primary purpose of everything we do in the church, including worship. We assume that traditional-form hymnals are irrelevant to today's culture. We assume that we have the absolute freedom to change or omit forms of worship; "Adiaphora, therefore freedom." And we assume that all form is neutral in relation to substance. The contention that form is neutral is a flawed assumption and it is misleading.

Yet it is assumed by some that the relationship between form and substance does not matter, and that this distinction between form and substance allows us to do anything we want in our worship practices. While the distinction between form and substance is a confessional concept, as I will demonstrate in what follows, we must not use this distinction to justify bad practices.

It is also assumed by others that form equals substance when we talk about liturgy, and that we must not separate form from substance. This assumption, however, cannot be demonstrated from Scripture or the Lutheran Confessions, and it leads to the mistaken conclusion that there can be only a single authentic liturgical form in the church. It is an assumption that originates from Roman Catholic and Eastern Orthodox Liturgical Theology. The approach taken by Scripture and the Lutheran Confessions is to make a clear distinction between form and substance.

The Lutheran Confessions make this distinction in their use of the Latin terms *accidens* and *substantia*. I will define these terms for you by sharing a quote from *Formula of Concord*, Solid Declaration, Article I on Original Sin from the *Book of Concord*.

> Among other considerations this is also an indisputable, incontrovertible axiom in theology, that each *substantia* or independent essence, insofar as

> it is a substance, is either God himself or a product and creation of God. . . . All scholars and intelligent people have always held to this: that whatever does not exist in and of itself or is not a part of another independent essence, but may change as it exists in something else, is not a *substantia* (that is, something self-subsistent), but is an *accidens* (that is, something contingent)." (*Formula of Concord*, Solid Declaration I.55)[1]

Substantia ("substance") is defined as the "essence" of a thing, while *accidens* ("accident") is defined as something that has the ability to change as it exists in relation to something else.

Let me illustrate this for you. The substance is hair. Hair is created by God. The accident is the length of the hair. Length of hair exists only in connection with hair. In other words, it is contingent on the existence of hair. You cannot have hair length if you do not have hair.

Another example: the substance is skin. Skin is created by God. The accident is the condition of the skin. Condition of one's skin exists only in connection with skin. It is contingent on there being skin. In other words, you cannot have a skin condition if you do not have skin.

One more example: the substance is fingernails. Fingernails are created by God. The accident is the length of the fingernails. Length of fingernails exists in connection with fingernails. That is, you cannot have fingernail length if you do not have fingernails.

What *Formula of Concord* Article I addresses is the relationship between human nature and original sin. The

1. For context see *Formula of Concord*, Solid Declaration I.54–62; see also *Formula of Concord*, Epitome I.23–25.

question is whether original sin is to be equated with human nature. The conclusion the *Formula of Concord* draws is that the substance is human nature. Human nature is created by God. It is created by God to be good and in a right relationship with him. The accident is original sin. Original sin exists only in connection with human nature. It is embedded in human nature, and it thoroughly corrupts our human nature, but it is itself not human nature. Original sin is not God, and it is not created by God.

To apply this concept and language to the church's liturgy, the substance is the Gospel and the sacraments (according to *Augsburg Confession* VII). The Gospel and the sacraments are given by God. The accident is liturgy (in the broad sense, i.e., ceremonies instituted by men). Liturgy in the broad sense is not given by God; it is given by the church. It exists in connection with the Gospel and the sacraments, and is contingent on the existence of the Gospel and the sacraments. Liturgy in the broad sense is the external expression of the Gospel in the church. It is the external form of the Gospel.

The Lutheran Confessions refer to the practice of "externals" when speaking of humanly instituted rites and ceremonies in liturgy. This is the *accidens* in the distinction between form and substance. We need to be clear about the biblical and confessional distinction between form and substance and make every effort not to confuse the two. In other words, the assumption that form equals substance is incorrect according to the Lutheran point of view.

Some have claimed that none of this matters. The only thing that matters is giving people what they want, with the goal of saving souls. I even heard a pastor some years ago say that anything goes as long as we are "getting them into heaven by the skin of their teeth." So we adopt American Evangelical contemporary forms uncritically. We taint our worship with decision theology. Or we do not administer the sacraments as they are given in Scripture. Informality, spontaneity, and feelings are what really matter. Don't tell me about the cross, because I don't think I need to be forgiven. Just give me "how to-s"—how to be a better parent, how to raise my children with the right values, how to live my life free of debt, how to retire with a big fat bank account by the time I'm fifty, how to suffer with a smile and a "praise the Lord" on my lips, how to ... how to ... how to .... Just don't tell me about the cross, and all that other depressing stuff. I get enough of that at work, or when I watch the news on TV.

Some have said that, even though a larger congregation may have multiple services, having the same liturgy in each of the services means that they are "worshiping together." The analogy of a restaurant is used. If I go to a specific restaurant on Saturday, and you go to the same restaurant on Sunday, we have a common basis for a conversation about the food we were served.

As appealing as this argument may seem, it is still a rationalization based on a flawed assumption. The flawed assumption is that the form must be the same, in order for us to have a unified worship. It is not the plates we eat from that matter most. It is the food that matters most. I can eat the same food on different forms of table service—fine china, ceramic, wood, plastic, or paper. I can even eat my food off the floor if I want to. So I can have the same purity of the Gospel and sacraments given according to God's Word, even if the forms of worship are different. What matters most is the food that nourishes. In the case of liturgy in the narrow sense, it is the food that nourishes with the hope and promise of eternal life.

But every care must be taken here. I may have the freedom to eat my food off the floor, or from paper or plastic, but is it always good for me to exercise this freedom? I may want everyone to clap and dance in worship.[2] But if the local culture frowns on clapping and dancing, then this is not edifying worship and I should not seek to impose clapping and dancing on my fellow worshipers. On the other hand, there may indeed be a local culture where clapping and dancing are actually expected of the worshiper. In which case, those who like clapping and dancing would fit right in.

The Apostle Paul wrote, "'All things are lawful,' but not all things are helpful. 'All things are lawful,' but not all things build up. Let no one seek his own good, but the good of his neighbor." (1 Corinthians 10:23–24) This is a principle the reformers repeatedly appealed to when they wrote about worship. So it is not just *my* personal choice about worship that matters most in the church. It is whether others in the church also desire to make the same changes in their worship practices. Do you see?

Lutheran assumptions about worship must be based on the simplest of guiding principles: Lutheran theology for Lutheran worship. The only recognized authorities for Lutheran theology and practice of worship are Scripture and the Lutheran Confessions. It is when we are faithful to adhere to this principle, that we will find ourselves to be in possession of the means to move beyond where we are. If our assumptions are

2. This is a hypothetical argument. In reality I am uncomfortable with clapping and dancing in worship because of the conservative culture of my Midwestern upbringing.

based on the simplest of guiding principles: Lutheran theology for Lutheran worship, then faithful methodology will follow, a topic to which we will turn next chapter.

SUMMARY POINTS

- Assumptions matter; so does the necessity to examine our assumptions in light of Scripture and the Lutheran Confessions.

- The most important assumptions about worship, according to Scripture and the Lutheran Confessions, begin by recognizing that the Gospel (justification) is at the center of worship and liturgy is *adiaphora*.

- Lutheran theology of worship distinguishes form and substance. This does not mean, however, that anything goes.

- It is not my personal opinion about worship that matters most. What matters most is edification of my neighbor. (1 Corinthians 10:23–24)

STUDY / DISCUSSION QUESTIONS

1. Why, if at all, is it necessary for us to be aware of our assumptions when it comes to life in general? When it comes to our point of view on worship? What would Socrates say? What would Scripture say? Can you think of other Scriptures that make this point? Why does this matter?

2. What are the most important assumptions about worship according to the Lutheran point of view? Why

are they so important? How can these assumptions be misused?

3. How can the confessional distinction between form and substance be abused with regard to worship? On the other hand, why is it a problem when we fail to make this distinction? How do the Lutheran Confessions help us to get it right?

4. When the Apostle Paul writes in 1 Corinthians 10:23–24 that "All things are lawful," what does he mean when he adds to this that "not all things are useful" and that "not all things build up"? How would you apply this to the conversation about worship? What does it mean for our relationships in the church, when we approach each other to have the conversation about worship?

5

More about Assumptions and Methodology

WE SAW in the previous chapter how the distinction between form and substance allows the church, at least in principle, to make changes in the way it worships. This begs the question, who has the confessional authority to make changes in the church's liturgy? Is it the pastor? Is it the board of elders? The worship committee? The voters assembly? Or is it the Synod in convention? The Commission on Worship? The faculty of our colleges, universities, and seminaries? I want to examine briefly here the question whether it is the local congregation or the larger church body that has the confessional authority and freedom to order liturgical rites and ceremonies in the church.

MORE ABOUT ASSUMPTIONS

In his classic work, *The Structure of Lutheranism*, Werner Elert discussed how the *Formula of Concord* combated the idea that by bringing about uniformity in liturgy the two opposing parties in the Reformation (the Lutherans and the Roman Catholics) could be brought into theological agreement. Elert wrote: ". . . the principle expressed by the Formula of Concord [is] 'that the community of God in every place and at every time [that is, in every local congregation] has the right, authority, and power to change, reduce, or increase' external customs (X, 9) . . . ."[1] The word the *Formula of Concord* uses, which is translated "community of God" and which Elert identified as the local congregation, is *Gemeine*.

Let's look at *Formula of Concord*, Solid Declaration, Article X, paragraph 9:

> Therefore, we believe, teach, and confess that the community of God [*Die Gemeine Gottes*] in every time and place has the right, power, and authority to change, reduce, or expand such practices according to circumstances [*nach derselben Gelegenheit*] in an orderly and appropriate manner, without frivolity or offense, as seems most useful, beneficial, and best for good order, Christian discipline, evangelical decorum, and the building up of the church.

There are two points that we can make about this passage. The first point is that the German phrase, *Die Gemeine Gottes*, which is translated "the community of God," refers to the local congregation. This is clearly demonstrated by the context of the passage quoted above, by parallel passages, and by synonyms of *Gemeine* in the Lutheran Confessions (like *Versamblung* in the *Large Catechism*, for example). This particular passage in *Formula of Concord* X demonstrates that the local congregation has the confessional authority and freedom to order its own humanly instituted rites and ceremonies in liturgy.

The other point I want to make about this passage is with regard to the German phrase, *nach derselben Gelegenheit*. This phrase means "according to its own circumstances." In addition to the correct understanding of *Gemeine* as the local con-

1. Werner Elert, *The Structure of Lutheranism*, trans. Walter E. Hansen (St. Louis: Concordia, 1962) 333.

gregation at Article X paragraph 9, *nach derselben Gelegenheit* further emphasizes the confessional authority of the local congregation to order its own rites and ceremonies in liturgy, "according to its own circumstances." If it were otherwise, the reformers would not have mentioned it.

I want to share with you one more passage from the Confessions to demonstrate this point. In *Formula of Concord*, Solid Declaration, Article X paragraph 25 we have the following:

> From this explanation everyone can understand what a Christian community[2] and every individual Christian, particularly pastors, may do or omit in regard to indifferent things without injury to their consciences, especially in a time when confession is necessary, so that they do not arouse God's wrath, do not violate love, do not strengthen the enemies of God's Word, and do not offend the weak in faith.

Both the German version which has *Gemein*, and the Latin version which has *unamquamque ecclesiam*, highlight the church's confession that it is the local congregation that has the confessional authority and freedom to order its own humanly instituted rites and ceremonies in liturgy. This confessional authority is not autonomy for the local congregation to do whatever it pleases. The local congregation does not exist in a vacuum. It exists in a relationship with other Lutheran churches. The local congregation, however, does have the confessional authority and genuine Gospel-freedom to order its own humanly instituted rites and ceremonies in liturgy, ac-

---

2. For "Christian community" the German version has *christlichen Gemein*; there's *Gemein* again; the Latin version has *unamquamque ecclesiam*.

cording to its own circumstances, for the building up of God's people in that place.

There is one further assumption I want to point out here (although there are far more than the space will allow). Does the unity of the church depend on all Lutheran congregations having the same liturgy? In my study of liturgy I intentionally read the sources with the honest expectation that I would find the reformers drawing a close connection between everyone having the same liturgical order and the unity of the church. In other words, I expected to find that the unity of the church depends on liturgical uniformity. And to be honest, I expected to find this connection everywhere, because in many present-day writings, blogs, and general discussions about liturgy, one can easily find numerous assertions about the unity of the church depending on uniformity of liturgy.

However, this connection is not made either in Scripture or in the sixteenth-century sources. In fact, it is explicitly written against, even in the church's confession at Article VII of the *Augsburg Confession*. Now, having said that, I should add this caveat. Uniformity of liturgical order is a desirable thing. It is good for the church. And it promotes harmony. But what I have found in my reading of the sources is that, while the reformers spoke of their desire for the church to have a uniform liturgy, along with that desire they were also honest about admitting the reality that this was not always possible, and that what mattered most and what was absolutely non-negotiable for the church was what they confessed in *Augsburg Confession* VII: unity in the Gospel and the sacraments. They strove for a certain level of uniformity in the outline of the service, but they also allowed for variety in the execution of the forms.

A FEW COMMENTS ABOUT METHODOLOGY

Now I want to say a little about our methodology when we speak and write about the church's worship. Just as we must always be up front about our assumptions, so we must always be up front about our methodology. There are two issues I would like to address regarding methodology. First we will look at selection of sources. Then we will look at how we read those sources.

Selection of sources must always begin with the assumption: Lutheran theology for Lutheran worship. If we claim we can take Roman Catholic or Eastern Orthodox points of view on liturgy, sanitize them, and give them a "Lutheran spin," then to be consistent, we must allow others to take Evangelical contemporary form, sanitize it, and give it a "Lutheran spin." The flip-side is just as true. If we adopt contemporary points of view on worship that do not have their origins in Lutheran theology, then we cannot criticize others for co-opting Roman Catholic or Eastern Orthodox points of view on worship.

We need to be clear about what precisely are the problems. On the contemporary end the problem is the uncritical adoption of contemporary forms. This taints our worship with license and false doctrine. So many contemporary worship songs focus on the feelings of the worshiper, make claims that the worshiper has chosen to worship God,[3] or contain the all-

3. Here the meaning of the third article of the Creed from Luther's Small Catechism is most helpful: "I believe that I cannot by my own reason or strength believe in Jesus Christ, my Lord, or come to Him; but the Holy Spirit has called me by the Gospel, enlightened me with His gifts, sanctified and kept me in the true faith. In the same way He calls, gathers, enlightens, and sanctifies the whole Christian church on earth, and keeps it with Jesus Christ in the one true faith. . . ."

too-generic references to "God" without any clear reference to Christ or what Christ did for us on the cross for us and for our salvation. This is so because the cross and forgiveness are not at the center of the theology of those who wrote the songs. Granted, there are a few well-written contemporary songs that are Christ-centered, Gospel-focused songs. But there are not nearly enough of these and they are not so easy to find.

The problem on the other end is our model of confession (which we will discuss in more detail in chapter 7). It is not the Lutheran model of confession to correct an error by confessing the error's opposite. When we adopt this model of confession, all that happens is we end up stumbling along in the ditch on the other side. So, selection of sources must begin with the assumption: Lutheran theology for Lutheran worship.

Which means this: we look to Scripture and the Lutheran Confessions *only* as our authoritative sources for our theology of worship. These are the only two sources that have the authority to define our theology of worship.

The second methodological issue has to do with how we read the sources. Texts have contexts. And reading texts in their contexts is a basic methodological principle. It is good methodology. Taking small passages out of their contexts to support our prior assumptions is misleading; it is a dangerous practice that contributes to the spiritual harm of God's flock. We must always be open to the text reshaping our assumptions, rather than forcing hard data into the Procrustean bed of our prior assumptions.

Let me illustrate this. Procrustes was a mythical creature who attacked innocent travelers and made them lie down in one of his two beds. If the traveler happened to be too long for the bed Procrustes chose, he would cut off the victim's limbs to fit the bed. If the innocent traveler was too short for the bed he chose, Procrustes would wrack (stretch) his victim's limbs to make them fit. We use the myth of Procrustes as a metaphor for criticizing bad methodology. It is a metaphor for beginning a study of a topic with a set of prior assumptions, and then forcing the hard data of the historical sources to fit the construct of our assumptions, rather than allowing the sources to reshape our understanding.

What follows is an example of how proof-texting changes the meaning of a text. A Lutheran author quoted Luther's *German Mass* in an essay some years ago. And I will begin my quote of the Lutheran author in the broader context of Luther's *German Mass*, and then I will indicate to you where the author's quote of the *German Mass* begins and ends. I do this in order to demonstrate how the author manipulated the text into saying something other than what Luther intended.

This is what Luther wrote in his *German Mass*:

> As far as possible we should observe the same rites and ceremonies, just as all Christians have the same baptism and the same sacrament [of the altar] and no one has received a special one of his own from God. That is not to say that those who already have good orders, or by the grace of God could make better ones, should discard theirs and adopt ours. For I do not propose that all of Germany should uniformly follow our Wittenberg order. Even heretofore the chapters, monasteries, and parishes were not alike in every rite. . . .

Now, the author's quote of the *German Mass* begins here: ". . . But it would be well if the service in every principality would be held in the same manner and if the order observed in a given city would also be followed by the surrounding towns and villages . . . ." This is where the author's quote of the *German Mass* stops. By pulling this small snippet out of its context, the author leaves the reader with the impression that in the *German Mass* Luther insisted on liturgical uniformity in all of Germany, by referring to "the service in every principality."

Now let's look at the rest of the context in Luther's words immediately following what we have just read. The same (partially-quoted!) sentence continues, ". . . whether those in other principalities hold the same order or add to it ought to be a matter of free choice and not of constraint." (Luther's *German Mass*) This part of the sentence, which is crucial for understanding Luther's complete thought, is left out of the quotation. It is the kind of proof-texting that misrepresents the sources in order to promote a particular assumption. And rather than letting the sources shape our assumptions, it is our assumptions that shape our methodology and our reading of the sources. But this is bad methodology driven by wrong assumptions.

I want to take just a few lines here to correct this misreading of Luther's *German Mass*. Between the thirteenth and nineteenth centuries German history must be understood in terms of smaller, geographically defined principalities. The history of Germany during this period is by and large the result of complex relationships between individual principalities, between the principalities and the Holy Roman Empire, and between the principalities and other foreign nations. It is also a history of numerous unfruitful efforts on the part of the principalities to arrive at a unified Germany. There was indeed some sense of there being a German nation, as Luther's comments in his *German Mass* demonstrate (Luther refers to "all of Germany"). However, historians estimate that there were between 350 and 390 principalities during this period. It was a very complicated political landscape.

According to Martin Luther, Philip Melanchthon, and Martin Chemnitz to varying degrees—Chemnitz more so—liturgical uniformity could be required in local contexts, according to principalities, but not imposed on the entire German nation, as we just saw in Luther's *German Mass*. In America today there is nothing like the German principalities of the sixteenth century. They could be slightly larger than a circuit, but smaller than a district. The closest analogy today to a principality would probably be a larger circuit, or maybe two or three smaller circuits combined. This is the extent to which the reformers were willing to require liturgical uniformity.

One natural objection to this reading of our history is that medieval peasants were subjected to a dull, base life of immobility. They were, by and large, confined to the boundaries of the lands on which they lived and labored. Their lives were subjected to the service of those who controlled the wealth. The labor was hard and the days were long. The objection might run along these lines: since sixteenth-century peasants were less mobile, they had less of an opportunity to worship in a neighboring congregation. Therefore uniformity of liturgy was not as much of an issue. On the other hand, today mobility is a way of life. We travel from city to city, from state to state, from country to country, in a matter of hours. Uniformity of liturgy is necessary for the unity of the church for this reason alone, so that God's people may recognize the worship of the church wherever they happen to be. This is how the objection might run.

There are two problems with this objection. First, it does not take into consideration the theological argument against the necessity of uniformity in *Augsburg Confession* VII and *Formula of Concord* X. Neither does it take into consideration what these two documents confess about the recognizable marks of the church—the Gospel and the sacraments apart from humanly instituted rites and ceremonies.[4]

The second problem we should have with this objection is that, while peasant immobility was the general rule, there was also a substantial minority in the landed nobility. This class wielded much power, was very mobile, moving freely between principalities and kingdoms, negotiated alliances, and did business. It would actually make more sense if local Lutheran principalities had desired liturgical uniformity with each other, in order to strengthen their collective position vis-à-vis the Holy Roman Empire and the Roman Catholic Church, both of which competed vigorously with the German principalities for wealth and resources. This, however, was not the case. While liturgical uniformity is mentioned in the sources as something that would be good for the principalities to aspire to, such uniformity was not considered necessary for the unity or the identity of the church as it is argued today. In fact, the historical record of Lutheran church orders from the sixteenth century demonstrates that there were more than 130 different Lutheran church orders in Germany alone from the time Luther first reformed the liturgy with his *Latin Mass* of 1523 until well into the 1550s.

4. On the Gospel and the sacraments being the only externally "recognizable" marks of the church, see *Apology of the Augsburg Confession* VII & VIII.5.

The point is this: proof-texting does nothing but get us into trouble. It is not the sharp tool we need to learn the lessons of church history. Proof-texting is a blunt instrument we use to hammer the square peg into the round hole. The bad methodology of proof-texting must never take the place of the good methodology of reading passages in their contexts. Let our opinions about worship be shaped by the sources, and not our reading of the sources be shaped by our opinions.

If our assumptions are based on the simplest of guiding principles: Lutheran theology for Lutheran worship, then faithful methodology will follow. To be faithful in our methodology means that we will not allow our prior assumptions to determine the outcome before we even begin our readings of the sources. Rather, good methodology will have the authoritative sources of our faith to shape our assumptions and determine the conclusions.

SUMMARY POINTS

- The local congregation has the confessional authority and freedom to order its own worship.

- This confessional authority and freedom for the local congregation, however, does not mean free license or "anything goes" in worship practices.

- While the local congregation exists in a relationship with other Lutheran congregations, the unity of the church does not depend on uniformity of liturgy.

- Proof-texting is bad methodology; it misrepresents the sources and is used to advance pre-conceived conclusions.

- Good methodology matters; reading texts in their contexts is good methodology.

- Luther and the other sixteenth-century reformers did not require liturgical uniformity on the scale of the entire German nation. They only required liturgical uniformity on the scale of the principality.

STUDY / DISCUSSION QUESTIONS

1. According to *Formula of Concord* Article X, who has the confessional authority to order the church's rites and ceremonies in worship? What does this mean for a congregation's collective identity with the larger Lutheran Church?

2. If the local congregation has the confessional authority and freedom to order its rites and ceremonies in liturgy according to its own circumstances as *Formula of Concord* X confesses, what are the boundaries? How far can we go? How far should we go?

3. Why is selection of sources important for a correct understanding of Lutheran theology and practice of liturgy?

4. Why is "proof-texting" a problem? What is a solution to the problem? Can you think of specific examples?

6

Worship As *Adiaphora*

HAVE YOU ever tried to make a decision, but did not quite know what was the right thing to do? Most of us will readily admit that at some point in our lives (maybe even more than once!) we have been here. It is called the proverbial "gray area."

What does it mean to say that liturgy is *adiaphora*? There is entirely too much confusion in the church today over the relationship between liturgy and *adiaphora*. Some think that, because liturgy is *adiaphora*, we can do anything we want: "Adiaphora, therefore freedom!" In response to this extreme abuse of the doctrine, others say that liturgy is not *adiaphora* at all: *leitourgia divina adiaphora non est*—"the divine liturgy is not adiaphora."

You recall from chapter 3 how the Lutheran Confessions make a distinction between liturgy in the narrow sense and liturgy in the broad sense. This distinction helps us to understand the difference between what is given by God and what is given by the church. This is the basic confessional framework for understanding the relationship between liturgy and *adiaphora*. Remember, liturgy in the narrow sense is the purity of the Gospel and the sacraments administered in accordance with the divine Word. Liturgy in the broad sense is all the humanly instituted rites and ceremonies that the church has added to the Gospel and the sacraments, all those things that are neither commanded nor forbidden by God, as *Formula of Concord* X defines *adiaphora*.

The *Formula of Concord* defines *adiaphora* as "ceremonies that . . . in themselves [are] indifferent matters neither commanded nor forbidden by God."[1] In other words, God's Word is silent on matters which in their nature are *adiaphora*.

Adiaphora is a Greek word.[2] It was used in Classical literature from Aristotle's Rhetoric and Metaphysics, to Epicurus, to Stoic philosophy referring to things neither good nor bad, to Cicero and Epictetus. The word *adiaphora* was used by Jewish writers of the first century, Philo of Alexandria and Flavius Josephus, and later by church historians like Eusebius of Caesarea. *Adiaphora* has a basic meaning of an undifferentiated middle ground. For example, Philo wrote in clear terms about the difference between good and evil, but he also used the term *adiaphora* to describe an ambiguous gray area between good and evil. In other words, the philosophers recognized that there were some things about which there was no divine instruction in the holy Scriptures. This is what they called *adiaphora*.

The reformers used a Latin word to translate the Greek word *adiaphora*. They used the Latin word *indifferens*, which has been translated into English as "indifferent matters." This is an unfortunate translation, because it leaves the impression that *adiaphora* are things that don't really matter all that much.

1. *Formula of Concord*, Epitome X.1–2; see also *Formula of Concord*, Solid Declaration X.1–3.

2. The singular form of the word is *adiaphoron*. The plural form is *adiaphora*.

Rather than "indifferent matters," the word *indifferens* in Latin means "things undifferentiated" by God, or better still, "things indistinguishable" with regard to a command or a prohibition of God. For the sake of good order in the church's worship, the reformers were clear that we should not treat *adiaphora* with indifference.

In his small but important book, *Luther's Liturgical Criteria and His Reform of the Canon of the Mass*, liturgical scholar Bryan Spinks wrote the following: "... while it is true that Luther regarded liturgical ceremonies as indifferent things (*adiaphora*), it is a mistake to interpret this to mean that Luther himself had no interest in them."[3] It is quite true that Luther was a very capable reformer of the church's liturgy, basing his entire approach on the doctrine of justification. Luther was also quite clear about the role that *adiaphora* played in liturgy.

In his 1525 work titled, *Against the Heavenly Prophets in the Matter of Images and Sacraments*,[4] Luther wrote:

> Teaching and doing are two things. I say, furthermore, that one should separate teaching and doing as far from each other as heaven from earth. Teaching belongs only to God. He has the right and the power to command, forbid, and be master over the conscience. However, to do and refrain from doing belongs to us so that we may keep God's commandment and teaching. Where doing or to refrain from doing is in question, and concerning which God has taught, commanded, and forbid-

3. Bryan D. Spinks, *Luther's Liturgical Criteria and His Reform of the Canon of the Mass*, Grove Liturgical Study No. 30 (Bramcote: Grove Books, 1982) 13; see also 22.

4. *American Edition of Luther's Works*, 40.129.

> den nothing, there we should permit free choice as
> God himself has done. Whoever though goes be-
> yond this by way of commandments or prohibition
> invades God's own sphere of action, burdens the
> conscience, creates sin and misery, and destroys all
> that God has left free and certain. In addition he
> expels the Holy Spirit with all his kingdom, work,
> and word, so that nothing but devils remain.

One thing is for certain. Luther can never be accused of being unclear about the concept of *adiaphora*.

The German word that translates *adiaphora* in the Lutheran Confessions is *Mitteldingen*. On the one hand there are those things commanded by God. On the other hand there are those things forbidden by God. Then there are all the things in the middle, *Mitteldingen*. These are the things that are neither commanded nor forbidden by God. This is what the Confessions refer to as *adiaphora*.

The formulators of the *Formula of Concord* constructed Article X on Church Ceremonies in the context of address-ing the division that had arisen in Lutheran churches over *adiaphora* between 1548 and 1577. Historians call this the Adiaphoristic Controversy. The opening statement of Article X reads: "A dispute also occurred among the theologians of the Augsburg Confession over ceremonies or ecclesiastical practices that are neither commanded nor forbidden in God's Word but that were introduced in the churches for the sake of good order and decorum."

The formulators of Article X composed five "Affirmative Theses" in order to confess their understanding of the nature of *adiaphora*. They placed these theses under the heading:

"The Proper, True Teaching and Confession concerning This Article." This is what the formulators wrote:

1. To settle this dispute, we unanimously believe, teach, and confess that ceremonies or ecclesiastical practices that are neither commanded nor forbidden in God's Word, but have been established only for good order and decorum, are in and of themselves neither worship ordained by God nor a part of such worship.

2. We believe, teach, and confess that the community of God [*die Gemein Gottes*] in every place and at every time has the authority to alter such ceremonies according to its own situation [*nach derselben Gelegenheit*], as may be most useful and edifying for the community of God [*der Gemeinen Gottes*].

This refers to more than just the church's freedom to keep what it has received of historic liturgical traditions from the past. It also demonstrates the formulators' clear sense that the local congregation has the confessional authority and freedom to change liturgical rites and ceremonies to address its changing times and circumstances for the sake of what is "most useful and edifying for the community of God."

Now, having said that, there is a caveat. The formulators have warned us that this freedom is not license. This is clear in the third Affirmative Thesis on *adiaphora*. "3. Of course, all frivolity and offense must be avoided, and special consideration must be given particularly to those who are weak in faith." In today's context defining what is frivolous and offensive is not so easy. One person's frivolity and offense is another person's edification. This is not an easy point to work out in present circumstances. But we must make every effort and be persistent, while erring always on the side of the Gospel, rather than on the side of the Law. The Gospel creates faith and edifies, while the Law always accuses and condemns.

Returning to what Article X teaches about *adiaphora*. Having confessed their positive theses on the nature of *adiaphora* and the church's freedom in its use of *adiaphora* in liturgy, the formulators then crafted their confession of *adiaphora* in the context of persecution:

> We believe, teach, and confess that in a time of persecution, when an unequivocal confession of faith is demanded of us, we dare not yield to the opponents in such indifferent matters [*Mitteldingen*]. For in such a situation it is no longer indifferent matters [*Mittelding*] that are at stake. The truth of the gospel and Christian freedom are at stake. The confirmation of open idolatry, as well as the protection of the weak in faith from offense, is at stake. In such matters we can make no concessions but must offer an unequivocal confession and suffer whatever God sends and permits the enemies of his Word to inflict on us.

This is the church's confession of *adiaphora* in a context of persecution.

In such a context, "the truth of the gospel," "Christian freedom," the necessity to avoid "confirmation of open idolatry," as well as "protection of the weak in faith" are all non-negotiable concerns "in a time of persecution." We have already seen how the local congregation has the Christian freedom to change its ceremonies in liturgy. Yet here freedom is curtailed in order to meet the requirements of confession in a context of persecution.

To apply this to today's context, we have this unfortunate tendency to split apart these four concerns about *adiaphora*, and then pit them against each other. Those who defend historic liturgical forms emphasize the truth of the Gospel and the necessity to avoid confirming open idolatry. Those who practice alternative or contemporary forms highlight Christian freedom and protecting the weak.

The solution to this thorny problem is to come together, like two sides of the same coin, to join our concerns for the sake of harmony and the edification of the church in the Gospel. This is a solution that is faithful to Scripture and the Confessions.

Having outlined their position on *adiaphora* in the context of persecution, the formulators then confessed that it is inappropriate for one church to condemn another because of differing practices in external ceremonies.

> We also believe, teach, and confess that no church should condemn another because the one has fewer or more external ceremonies not commanded by God than the other has when otherwise there is unity with the other in teaching and all the articles of faith and in the proper use of the holy sacraments . . . .

No church should condemn another. I was born and raised in the rural Midwest, near a large Midwestern city. I still have many family and friend connections back home, and what I hear from them is that Lutheran pastors are preaching from their pulpits against other Lutheran pastors and congregations in their circuits who include contemporary forms in their worship. These are Lutheran congregations that these pastors are not called to serve or oversee, yet for whatever reason they feel compelled to preach against them. It is our confession that "No church should condemn another because the one has fewer or more external ceremonies not commanded by God than the other has." So why are we today laboring beneath each other's mutual condemnations and hindering God's purpose for his church? Over *adiaphora*?

Along with affirmative theses, Article X also makes several antithetical statements on *adiaphora*. Let me share a couple of these with you.

> Therefore, we reject and condemn as incorrect and contrary to God's Word: . . . When anyone teaches that human commands and prescriptions in the church are to be regarded in and of themselves as worship ordained by God [*Gottesdienst*] or a part of it. When anyone imposes such ceremonies, commands, and prescriptions upon the community of God with coercive force as if they were necessary, against its Christian freedom, which it has in external matters. Likewise, when anyone teaches that in a situation of persecution, when public confession is necessary, one may comply or come to terms with the enemies of the holy gospel in these indifferent matters [*Mitteldingen*] and ceremonies. (Such actions serve to damage God's truth.) Likewise, when such external ceremonies and indifferent matters [*Mitteldingen*] are abolished in a way that suggests that the community of God is not free at all times, according to its specific situation, to use one or more of these ceremonies in Christian freedom, as is most beneficial to the church.

These antithetical statements reinforce the affirmative theses that *adiaphora* are not of the essence of liturgy, that freedom is essential as circumstances warrant, and that no church should condemn another with regard to these matters.

To provide you with a bit of the history behind Article X, the debate among Lutherans between 1548 and 1577 (the Adiaphoristic Controversy) over *adiaphora* and confession was heated and embittered, in much the same way the worship wars today are heated and embittered. The debate revolved around how the Lutherans would respond to Roman Catholic pressures to reinstate specific liturgical ceremonies which had been removed from the liturgies of Lutheran churches. This pressure by the Roman Catholics came in the form of a document known as the Augsburg Interim.

The Augsburg Interim was an imperial decree of Emperor Charles V in the wake of his army's defeat of the Schmalkaldic League of Lutheran forces in 1547. You might say the Interim was one of the spoils of war enjoyed by the imperial and papal alliance. The Augsburg Interim imposed uniformity of *adiaphora* on Lutheran churches that had reformed their local liturgies according to the teachings of the *Augsburg Confession*. The Interim reinstated rites that contradicted the biblical teaching of justification, such as exorcism at Baptism, the sacrifice of the Mass, and the Corpus Christi procession. What the Interim in fact did, was to divide the Lutherans over the doctrine of *adiaphora*, launching the Adiaphoristic Controversy. Two specific factions were at odds: the Philippists and the Gnesio-Lutherans.

The Philippists, who were also called the Interimists, followed the lead of Philip Melanchthon. The Philippists responded to the Roman Catholic pressure of the Augsburg

Interim, published the 15th of May 1548, with the compromise of the Leipzig Interim in December of that same year. In the Leipzig Interim the Philippists proposed that certain compromises in *adiaphora* could be granted by the Lutherans to the Roman Catholics.

The Gnesio-Lutherans, or the so-called "genuine Lutherans," were anti-Interimists. Led by Matthias Flacius, the Gnesio-Lutherans of Magdeburg vehemently opposed the compromise of the Leipzig Interim. They argued that the restoration of visible *adiaphora* (the paschal candle, for example) in liturgies that had been reformed, would signal to the lay people that the Lutherans had capitulated to the demands of Rome, and that the Gospel had been lost in the church. Flacius insisted that *adiaphora* cease to be *adiaphora* in a case of confession and persecution. This controversy went on for nearly thirty years, during which time the extreme polemics of the anti-Interimists did nothing to foster fraternal understanding among the Lutherans. That is, until Martin Chemnitz and the more centrist leaning Loyal Lutherans entered the fray and sorted out the mess.

The Centrists were much more cool-headed and consistent in their confession. These Centrists, Jakob Andreae, Nicholas Selnecker, Andrew Musculus, Christopher Körner, David Chytraeus, and Martin Chemnitz, would eventually be responsible for crafting the *Formula of Concord* for the Lutheran Church. The Lutheran churches recognized confession of the truth and freedom of the Gospel in the theological discourse of the Loyal Lutherans. The churches also recognized that this was a way which made for peace. This was so because the position of the Loyal Lutherans was tainted by neither of the extremes. Clearly these three positions by analogy may be identified with the three positions in the church today: two extremes with a large, silent (and suffering) center.

Flacius' position, that *adiaphora* cease to be *adiaphora* in a case of confession and scandal, continues to persist in the Lutheran Church today. It continues to persist in spite of the fact that it was written out of the *Formula of Concord* and is not the confession of the church. It is the church's confession that *adiaphora* "in their nature and essence are and remain in and of themselves free,"[5] and not that *adiaphora* cease to be *adiaphora* in certain circumstances.

Regardless of the circumstances, the nature of *adiaphora* remains the same. An *adiaphoron* is and always will be an *adiaphoron*, since the silence of God's Word can never be changed. When someone imposes or requires *adiaphora* as if they were necessary, or in such a way that the Gospel and Christian freedom are at stake, then *adiaphora* must be used, or not used, in such a way that the truth of the Gospel and Christian freedom are clearly and unequivocally confessed. *Adiaphora* remain *adiaphora* even in the context of confession.

Flacius' position was an extreme reaction to the Philippist position of compromise. It is a flawed model of confession in which an error is corrected by confessing the error's opposite, a model that was written out of the *Formula of Concord*, but one that is still adhered to by some in the Lutheran Church today. What is called for is clarification of the church's teaching of confession and how this relates to *adiaphora* in liturgy. We will discuss this in the next chapter.

---

5. *Formula of Concord*, Solid Declaration X.14.

SUMMARY POINTS

- The ancient definition of *adiaphora* is an undifferentiated middle ground between good and evil, the proverbial gray area.

- The definition of *adiaphora* as applied to worship in *Formula of Concord* X is that which is neither commanded nor forbidden by God.

- The Adiaphoristic Controversy (1548–1577) between the Philippists and the Gnesio-Lutherans, which was eventually sorted out by the more centrist-leaning Loyal Lutherans, helped define the church's teaching on *adiaphora* in the *Formula of Concord*.

- The definition of *adiaphora* in the Lutheran Confessions maintains that *adiaphora* "are and remain in and of themselves free," contrary to Matthias Flacius who insisted that *adiaphora* cease to be *adiaphora* under certain circumstances.

STUDY / DISCUSSION QUESTIONS

1. How was *adiaphora* defined by ancient authors? How is it defined in *Formula of Concord* Article X? Why is this important for our discussion of worship today?

2. What does it mean to have Christian freedom in the use of liturgical ceremonies? When do we cross the line between freedom and license in our worship practices? Is it possible to avoid this? How?

3. What does *Formula of Concord* X mean when it says "…all frivolity and offense must be avoided, and special consideration must be given particularly to those who are weak in faith." Based on your own observations and/or experience, what do you think constitutes "frivolity and offense" in today's context? How would you give "consideration … to those who are weak in faith"? Remember to choose your words carefully, in order to have a respectful conversation with the one who might disagree with you.

7

Worship As Confession

IN THE Gospel according to Matthew we have the Word of the Lord: ". . . everyone who confesses me before men, I also will confess him before my Father who is in heaven, but whoever denies me before men, I also will deny him before my Father who is in heaven." (Matthew 10:32–33, my translation; see also Romans 10:8–10 and Philippians 2:9–11)

There are two uses of the word "confess" in the Bible. One use of the word confess, the one that is familiar to most of us, is to confess sin. (Leviticus 16:21; Psalm 32:5; James 5:16; 1 John 1:9) We confess our sins to God, and we confess our sins to each other, always with the goal of seeking forgiveness of our sin and reconciliation. The second use of the word "confess" in the Bible is less familiar to most people in the church, but it is just as important. This use of the word confess is to make a declarative statement of what we believe. For example, we "confess" our Christian faith in the words of the Creed. According to Matthew 10:32–33, Jesus calls us to confess him openly to the world (see also Philippians 2:11). Worship is one way we do this.

What we speak and sing in worship proclaims (confesses) openly to the world the truth of Christ as this is given in Scripture. If what we speak and sing in worship does not proclaim (or confess) the truth as it is given in Scripture (because the song or hymn has been tainted by false teaching), then we are not confessing the Christ of Scripture. When we do not confess the Christ of Scripture, we are really confessing a Christ of our own making (see Matthew 16:13–14). Then we have crossed over into the scary realm of idolatry, and we all know where this leads in the end. If we use a worship song or hymn that incorrectly confesses Christ (decision theology, for example), then we need to be more careful about choosing songs and hymns in our worship that are faithful to confess the Christ of Scripture.

THE LUTHERAN CONCEPT OF WORSHIP AS CONFESSION

The Lutheran church is a confessing church. "We believe, teach, and confess" is the preamble of the church's confessions in the *Book of Concord*. Confession is of the essence of Christian faith. In the *Apology of the Augsburg Confession* Philip Melanchthon identified the marks of the church as "Word, confession of faith, and sacraments." (*Apology* VII & VIII.3) Melanchthon also wrote in the *Apology* that "No faith is firm that does not show itself in confession." (*Apology* IV.385) Confession is of the essence of the church. Confession and church go together. They cannot be separated.

The first and most important element of the church's confession is the Gospel, justification by grace alone through faith alone for Christ's sake. **(See Figure-2)** Jesus Christ crucified and risen from the dead, living among his people, delivering the forgiveness of sin in the church's worship, through the pure proclamation of the Gospel and the right administration of the sacraments—this is the most important element of the church's confession.

Figure-2: The Lutheran Concept of Worship As Confession

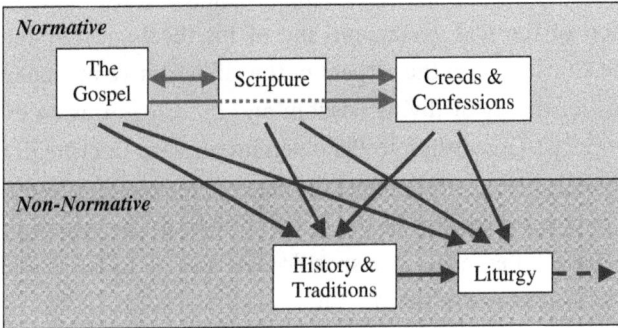

The Gospel is the good news of Jesus Christ, the crucified Son of God and living Savior, the Lord of Scripture who has forgiven our sin. Jesus is both God and man, fully human and fully divine, sent by God the Father and revealed by God the Holy Spirit. Christianity is a Trinitarian faith, the central doctrine of which is the Gospel of the crucified Messiah. Christ's righteousness is given in exchange for our unrighteousness. His life was given on the cross as a ransom for our lives, and in this way God has been reconciled to us and we are given to be coheirs of eternal life with Christ in heaven.

The Gospel is non-negotiable. It norms and informs our reading of sacred Scripture. Scripture is likewise non-negotiable. It is the only source and norm of doctrine in the church. ". . . from childhood you have been acquainted with the sacred writings, which are able to make you wise for salvation through faith in Christ Jesus. All Scripture is breathed out by God." (2 Timothy 3:15–17)

Historically, differences over specific doctrines have arisen out of different approaches to interpreting Scripture. In the second century Marcion scissored-and-pasted the "God of the Old Testament" out of his theological system. The Gnostics read the serpent of the fall narrative in Genesis 3 as a revealer of divine wisdom and the Creator as an evil demiurge. (According to Plato demiurges were intermediary heavenly beings who created the material universe.) These are differences that drive at the heart of biblical Christian faith. To have differences over specific doctrines is to be at odds over the essence of the church.

Consequently, the Creeds were crafted as interpretive keys which unlock the meaning of Scripture and which outline the essence of the church as that community in which the Scriptures are rightly interpreted. As the church actively confesses the truth and freedom of the Gospel when it experiences persecution and false doctrine, it both preserves and articulates its orthodox identity. This is the essence of confession.

The church confesses the three Ecumenical Creeds—the Nicene Creed, the Apostles' Creed, and the Athanasian Creed—and the 1580 *Book of Concord*. The *Book of Concord* contains the teachings of the Bible as confessed by the sixteenth-century Lutheran churches. These teachings are in catholic continuity with the historic Christian faith.[1] They are an accurate exposition of Scripture, which is why they continue to be normative sources for the church's theology and practice of worship today. Because the Confessions are an accurate exposition of holy

1. On this point see the Catalogue of Testimonies at the end of the *Book of Concord*.

Scripture, and because the Confessions are in complete agreement with Scripture, they are normative.

For something to be "normative," or for something to be a "norm," means that it is an authoritative standard by which the truth or accuracy of other things is measured. For example, to safeguard the accuracy of a football official's calls on the field, a rulebook has been adopted. If a call is in question, the rulebook is examined (and trusted) to provide the final word.

With regard to worship, these three, and these three only (the Gospel, Scripture, and Creeds & Confessions), are normative for the church. In other words, these are the authoritative standard of teaching to which we hold all pastors and teachers of the church. These are the only authoritative standards we have for worshiping as Lutherans.[2]

These normative elements of the church's confession constitute a boundary, outside of which the church's history and traditions play a limited role in the church's confession. History and tradition are normed by the Gospel. They are normed by Scripture. And they are normed by the Creeds and the Lutheran Confessions. History and traditions play a valuable role in terms of their contribution toward our fuller understanding of the church's faith and life. We value the church's history and traditions, but we do not overestimate them. The church's history and traditions are non-normative elements of the church's confession.

Liturgical traditions are also non-normative elements of the church's confession. Liturgy is normed by the Gospel. It is normed by Scripture. And liturgy is normed by the Creeds and the Lutheran Confessions. These are the only normative

2. See *Formula of Concord*, Epitome, Rule and Norm 1–8 and *Formula of Concord*, Solid Declaration, Rule and Norm 1–20.

authorities for shaping our theology and practice of worship, the only authorities. As liturgy is normed in this way by the Gospel, by Scripture, and by the Creeds & Confessions, liturgy is endowed with the gifts of God in the way of God's Word as Law and God's Word as Gospel. Equipped with this Word for the delivery of the gifts in the Gospel and the sacraments, liturgy confesses the Christ of Scripture.

The Apostle Paul wrote to the Christians of Corinth: "For Jews demand signs, and Greeks seek wisdom, but we preach Christ crucified, a stumbling block to Jews and folly to Gentiles, but to those who are called, both Jews and Greeks, Christ the power of God and the wisdom of God." (1 Corinthians 1:22–24)

Liturgy is informed by the church's history and traditions. We learn from the past. And we receive from the past many excellent humanly instituted rites and ceremonies, or liturgy in the broad sense. And in this way we rejoice in what is given by the church.

Liturgy is also informed by the unique cultural needs of the local congregation for edification in the Gospel. This point should be neither overstated nor simply dismissed.

As we have already seen, the local congregation has the confessional authority and freedom to order its own ceremonies in worship. This freedom, however, is not an unleashed autonomy. The local congregation is not normative in and of itself. When ordering its own ceremonies according to its own circumstances (*nach derselben Gelegenheit*), the local congregation must rely upon the normative authorities of the Gospel, Scripture, and the Creeds & Confessions. For the sake of harmony the local congregation also must take into consideration its identity within the larger Christian community. To ignore (or simply to dismiss) the larger context of the church's history and traditions demonstrates a *hubris* that our predecessors made every effort to avoid. (Does anyone remember what *hubris* means anymore?)

The local congregation is also part of a larger identity called the body of Christ. This is why, when the Apostle Paul traveled among the churches of Asia Minor and Greece, he appealed to their sense of fellowship (*koinōnia*), to motivate these local congregations to assist in alleviating the poverty and suffering of the churches in Judea. (Acts 11:27–30; 12:25; 24:17; 2 Corinthians 8–9) The local congregation has the confessional authority and freedom to order its own rites and ceremonies in worship. But consideration must be given to its participation in a larger fellowship of churches. The local congregation does not have unbridled license to do whatever it pleases. And it does not have the authority to impose its own practices on other congregations.

Ultimately, we are not slaves to our past. The church must be open to the leading of the Holy Spirit in the present and in the future. We have already seen this passage from Luther's *Latin Mass*, but it bears repeating: "The Scriptures prescribe nothing in these matters, but allow freedom for the Spirit to act according to his own understanding as the respective place, time, and persons may require it." This leaves open the possibility that in the present as well as in the future there can be the creation and use of new forms in the church's liturgy. German Lutheran scholar Peter Brunner once wrote: "But it would likewise register contempt for spiritual gifts if the church would decline to avail itself of hymns that are born in the congregation today simply because they are new or because their artistic style will not fit into a traditional pattern."[3]

We have reached the point where our theology of confession gives us a clearer understanding of our theology of worship. The church's history and traditions, and liturgy, while they constitute different ways of engaging in the act of confessing, these are non-normative elements of the church's confession. The reason I highlight this point is because there are some who treat worship as if the church's history and traditions and liturgy are on the same normative level as Scripture. But again, this is a misreading of our history in order to justify a wrong model of confession—to correct an error by confessing the error's opposite. And we must import non-Lutheran theology of worship from Roman Catholicism and Eastern Orthodoxy in order to do this, which violates the simple rule: Lutheran theology for Lutheran worship.

Our theology of confession further reveals that the uncritical adoption of contemporary forms from non-Lutheran sources is just as problematic. There are many contemporary resources from which to draw, and yet so few of them confess the Gospel in its truth and purity. Fair criticisms of such uncritical adoption of worship forms from non-Lutheran sources are justified.

It is also inappropriate for anyone to insist that, if we want the church to grow, a congregation must adopt contemporary forms of worship. This argument is based on the flawed premise that external forms, rather than the Holy Spirit working through the Gospel and the sacraments, are

3. *Worship in the Name of Jesus*, trans. M.H. Bertram (St. Louis: Concordia, 1968) 267–68.

what make the church grow. (Mark 4:26–29; 1 Corinthians 3:5–7) It is equally inappropriate for anyone to insist that only traditional forms of worship may be used in the church. Worship forms, whether traditional or contemporary, have no normative authority whatsoever.

What matters most, and what is absolutely non-negotiable, are the purity of the Gospel and the sacraments given in accordance with God's Word, regardless of the external form we wrap them in. Should we be concerned about false teaching in contemporary forms? Absolutely. But we should be equally concerned about false teaching in traditional forms. And we are. Which is why we are careful to sing only those hymns (and songs) that are faithful to the Gospel and the sacraments as these have been given by Christ.

APPLYING THE LUTHERAN MODEL OF CONFESSION

We have come to the point where we now have the proper tools to discuss how to apply the Lutheran model of confession to our theology and practice of worship. How do we put our confession into practice? In the Lutheran Church–Missouri Synod today there is the distinct tendency to follow a model of confession that attempts to correct an error by confessing the error's opposite. The obvious application to the topic of worship wars is that the Liturgical-Repristination point of view wrongly elevates historic liturgical traditions to a normative status in order to confess the opposite of contemporary worship.

I use the word "wrongly" in the most circumspect of ways. Historic liturgical forms are good for the church. They are good for the church and they should be appreciated and upheld. However, when we misread our history and give historic liturgical traditions a normative status, a status that our sixteenth-century predecessors went to great lengths not to give these traditions, this too is problematic. I am not sure where this wrong model of confession comes from. I have not found it in Scripture, the Lutheran Confessions, or in any of the writings of Luther, Melanchthon, or Chemnitz. It could be simply a hold-out of the old school of Matthias Flacius from the Adiaphoristic Controversy between 1548 and 1577. Or I wonder whether this model of confession is a remnant of Lutheran Church–Missouri Synod history, with roots going back to nineteenth-century German Pietism. Maybe it is a complex combination of the two. Regardless, to correct an error by confessing the error's opposite is not the Lutheran model of confession. One problem with such a model is that, instead of correcting the error, another error is created and we only end up in the ditch on the other side. Martin Chemnitz was critical of this method of confessing in his *Examination of the Council of Trent*.

In his *Examination* Chemnitz refers to the third-century Bishop Dionysius of Alexandria. Dionysius tried to correct the Trinitarian errors of Sabellius by adopting certain opposite Trinitarian errors that were similar to those of the later fourth-century Anomoeans (who followed the teachings of Arius). Sabellius claimed that the Son was the physical manifestation of the Father, and that they were in effect one and the same person (a form of modal monarchianism of northern Africa). In response Dionysius claimed that the Son was of an entirely different nature from the Father.

Martin Chemnitz quotes Basil of Caesarea's opinion of Dionysius: "I am accustomed therefore to compare [Dionysius] to an orchardist who wants to straighten the crooked shape of a sapling and then departs from the golden mean to err in the opposite direction by bending it too much."[4]

Basil also said of Dionysius: ". . . he is carried away unawares by his zeal into the opposite error. . . . he exchanges one mischief for another, and diverges from the right line of doctrine." If this is our model of confession, to correct an error by confessing the error's opposite, then we should not be surprised that we are bending the sapling too far, or that we are stumbling along in the ditch on the other side.

Neither is it our model of confession to make no confession at all. This model of confession is to have the truth, but because we are afraid that someone might disagree with us, we keep the truth to ourselves.

This is what Chemnitz wrote in his *Iudicium*: ". . . Christian piety requires not hypocrisy in external appearance (so that you can imagine that everything is right in your heart for a time), but a straightforward confession. For what would confession be, if it were permitted openly on the one hand to feign external appearance while on the other hand to think your confession privately?" Just as correcting an error by confessing the error's opposite is not the Lutheran model of confession, so also to have no confession at all is not the Lutheran model. So, what is the Lutheran model of confession?

4. *Examination of the Council of Trent* I, trans. Fred Kramer (St. Louis: Concordia, 1978) 262–63.

It is simply this: To confess straight ahead the truth and freedom of the Gospel. It is not a reactionary model, and it does not import non-Lutheran theology in order to make its point. It is simple. It is biblical. And it is Lutheran. Let me illustrate this with a passage from the *Formula of Concord*.

In the Affirmative Theses of Article X on *adiaphora*, the formulators gave us this model of confession: ". . . we should witness an unequivocal confession and suffer in consequence what God sends us and what he lets the enemies inflict on us." (*Formula of Concord*, Epitome X.6) This is our model of confession: straightforward, unequivocal confession.

The nature of the church's confession is such that it is given by God. Liturgy is one expression of the church's confession in the local congregation. Liturgy is also one of the non-normative elements of the church's confession. This is clarified when we are careful about our theology of confession, distinguishing what is normative from what is not normative, what is given by God from what is given by the church. At this point we have a solid basis for understanding our theology of worship, to which we will turn in the next chapter.

SUMMARY POINTS

- The only normative elements of the church's confession according to the Lutheran point of view are the Gospel, Scripture, and Creeds & Confessions.

- The Lutheran concept of confession also includes the worship of the local congregation, but only in a non-normative sense.

- It is not the Lutheran model of confession to correct an error by confessing the error's opposite; when we adopt this model of confession we only end up bending the sapling too far or stumbling along in the ditch on the other side.

- The Lutheran model of confession is to confess straight ahead the truth and freedom of the Gospel.

STUDY / DISCUSSION QUESTIONS

1. What is confession? Why is it important for the Christian to understand what it means to confess? Before you answer, first read Matthew 10:32–33 and Romans 10:8–10.

2. What are the only normative elements of the church's confession? Where is worship (i.e., liturgy) in relation to these normative elements? What does that mean for our understanding of worship?

3. Read 1 Corinthians 11:26. In what sense does participating in the worship of the local congregation also constitute a public confession of the Gospel to the world? Why is it important that any worshiper have a correct understanding of the Sacrament before participating in it?

4. Read Mark 4:26–29. Then read 1 Corinthians 3:5–7. Are we able to assume that we know precisely what it is that causes the church to grow? Who causes the church to grow? How? Some have said that the church must abandon traditional liturgy and in its place use contemporary worship, or the church will not grow. In light of the Scriptures you just read, *what would be a proper biblical response to this point of view*?

5. When someone insists that a congregation "must" worship only in contemporary forms, or someone else insists on only traditional forms of worship, *what might be the proper confessional response to such impositions*? In other words, how does our model of confession inform our practice? Hint: Do we correct an error by confessing the error's opposite? Or do we confess straight ahead the truth and the freedom of the Gospel? What does this mean for our conversation about worship in the church today? What would it look like in practice? Remember to craft your answer with respect for the person who might disagree with you.

8

Lutheran Theology for Lutheran Worship

IF I want to make cupcakes, would I follow the recipe for an omelet? Or if I want to knit a sweater, would I follow the blueprints for building a house? How about this one, if I want to teach my son to fish, would I take him to a football game? The answer to all of these questions would be, Of course not! By the same token we should not use non-Lutheran theologies of worship to shape our Lutheran way of worship.

Here I will give you detailed descriptions of the most important elements of our theology of worship, which I hope will be useful to you. And as I have stated before, the theology of worship presented here is based on the simple principle: Lutheran theology for Lutheran worship.

Lutheran theology of worship is not a reworked system taken over from Eastern Orthodox or Roman Catholic Liturgical Theology, which hold the liturgical traditions of the church to be on the same normative level as sacred Scripture, sometimes even above Scripture. Neither is it a Lutheran theology of worship to adopt uncritically American Evangelical contemporary worship forms. As we saw in the previous chapter, Lutheran theology (and practice) of worship is based on the only sources we recognize as authoritative for the church—the Gospel, Scripture, and the Creeds & Confessions.

Lutheran theology of worship distinguishes what is given by God from what is given by the church. (**See Figure-3**) Liturgy in the narrow sense must be distinguished from liturgy in the broad sense, the Gospel and the sacraments on the one hand, and humanly instituted rites and ceremonies on the other. This is consistent with *Augsburg Confession* VII and *Formula of Concord* X. Lutheran theology of worship also begins by assuming all that has gone into our Lutheran theology of confession.

Figure-3: Lutheran Theology for Lutheran Worship

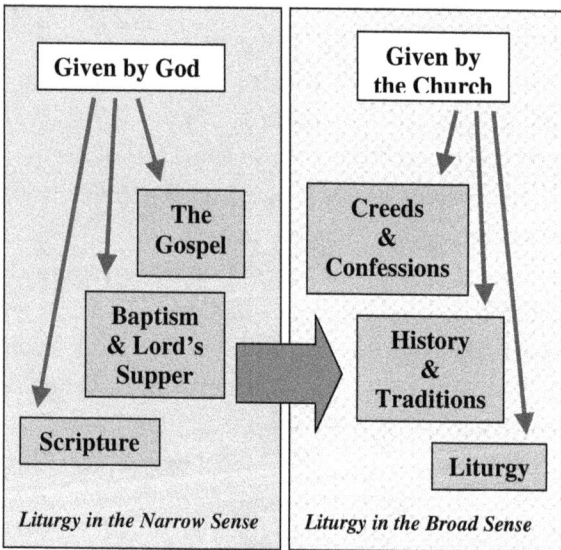

ASPECTS OF LUTHERAN WORSHIP
THAT ARE GIVEN BY GOD

The essence of Lutheran worship is the Gospel, justification by grace alone through faith alone for Christ's sake, the forgiveness of all sin in the crucified and risen Lord. All that is done in worship is done so that the Gospel is proclaimed and extolled and God's people are given the forgiveness of sins. Lutheran worship is steeped in the theology of the cross. The proclamation of Christ's crucifixion and resurrection for the forgiveness of sins in sermon, sacraments, and ceremonies is the non-negotiable essence of the church's worship.

God also gives us his precious sacraments: Holy Baptism and the Lord's Supper. Baptism is the washing of the Holy Spirit in the water with the Word. The Lord's Supper is the true body and blood of Christ in, with, and under bread and wine.

Scripture is also of the essence of worship. Luther once wrote: "What is changed according to God's Word is no innovation." It is not surprising that almost the entire liturgy, in its historic-traditional forms, reflects the church's faithful use of biblical texts in its proclamation and praise. These three are given by God: Holy Gospel, Holy Sacraments, Holy Scripture.

What is given by God norms what is given by the church. Liturgy in the narrow sense, given by God, norms liturgy in the broad sense, given by the church.

ASPECTS OF LUTHERAN WORSHIP
THAT ARE GIVEN BY THE CHURCH

Creeds and Confessions are given by the church. These are not just historic relics. They are authoritative documents that norm our theology of worship.

The church's history and traditions flow from the church's experience through time. The church's history and traditions are not given by God. They consist of a wide variety of experiences and thinking in the church—from the writings of popes, church fathers, councils, and locally developed liturgies, to the writings of our theological predecessors, their personal correspondences, biblical commentaries, theological treatises, and sermons.

These traditions are not given by God. They are given by the church as local culture and circumstances required them for the edification of the church. The role of the church's history and traditions is such that these give a fuller self-awareness to the church. Traditions suggest reasonable limits within which the local congregation understands itself to have both the confessional authority and the Gospel freedom to order its own liturgical rites and ceremonies.

And finally liturgy, all the humanly instituted rites, ceremonies, and traditions in the church. Liturgical traditions varied widely in different locations and at different times, and it would be an oversimplification to suggest that there is a single direct line of development from the time of the apostles down to our own day.

Liturgical traditions are not given by God; they are given by human beings in the church. Bishops, presbyters, deacons, and lay people gifted by God composed liturgical texts and taught them to the people. And this composition and instruction took place in the context of specific theological reflection, and many times this reflection was accompanied by heated theological debate in real historical contexts.

We learn from Scripture and the Lutheran Confessions that liturgy in the narrow sense is given by God to the church—

the Gospel and the sacraments. This is non-negotiable. This is the foundational expression of the church's worship, on which the community of God is free to build its sanctified response with humanly instituted rites and ceremonies.

We also learn from the Lutheran Confessions that liturgy in the broad sense is given by the church—all the humanly instituted rites, ceremonies, and traditions. Liturgy in the broad sense consists of a faith community's sanctified reception and extolling of the Gospel in its response to God in canticles, hymns, prayers, and joyful praise. This is not a prescribed form of worship. Rather, it is worship that freely responds to God's Gospel grace with the reception of all his gifts in Word and Sacrament. We rejoice in the beauty of the church's liturgy, and we revel in its greatness, but we do not overestimate its importance. Lutheran theology for Lutheran worship.

A MODEL FOR WORSHIPING
AS LUTHERANS

Now we turn to the issue of putting our theology into practice. Here I will give you concrete tools, a specific set of criteria for critiquing worship forms. Most Lutherans today either focus on what other denominations are doing with contemporary worship with very little if any critical reflection, or we take the do-not-handle, do-not-taste, do-not-touch approach to contemporary worship, which frankly is not helpful at all. What I will do instead is present a model for worshiping as Lutherans, which is essentially a framework for applying our theology of worship to our practice. **(See Figure-4)**

Figure-4: A Model for Worshiping As Lutherans

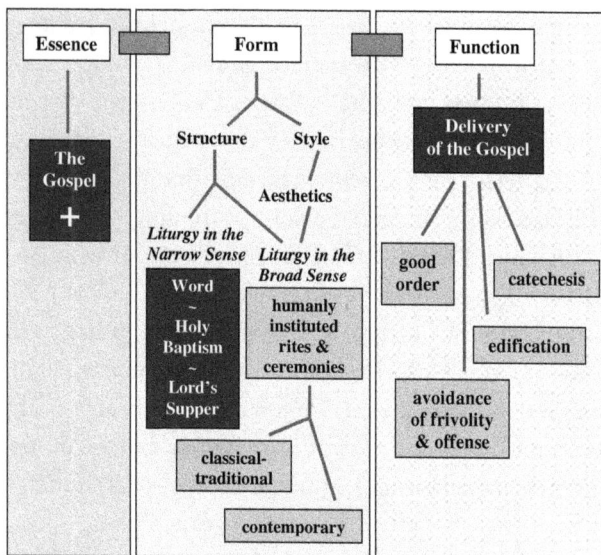

Keeping in mind the simple principle, Lutheran theology for Lutheran worship, how we worship as Lutherans may be viewed in terms of this basic model. Our Lutheran theology of worship is made up of the following three basic elements: essence, form, and function. Let me break this down for you.

The first basic aspect of the church's liturgy is its essence. What is the essence of Lutheran liturgy? To what does the liturgy refer? What is its core, central, primary message? The essence of the church's liturgy is the Gospel. And as I have already explained, the Gospel is this and only this, that our merciful God gave his Son to be crucified on a cross to pay the penalty for our sin, that Jesus suffered and shed his blood for us, to redeem us lost and condemned creatures.

The essence of Lutheran liturgy is the Triune God delivering his Gospel-gift. The Gospel is the means God uses to deliver to us the forgiveness of sins in the cross and resurrection of Christ. This is the confessional non-negotiable of Lutheran liturgy. With Article XV of the *Apology of the Augsburg Confession* we confess that "the chief worship of God is to preach the gospel." This is the essence of Lutheran worship—Christ crucified for the forgiveness of sins. The Gospel in its truth and purity is the essence of our worship. This is the first, and ultimately the most important, element in the model for worshiping as Lutherans.

The second basic element of the church's liturgy is its form. Liturgy must be delivered in some form. This is a point that has received an enormous amount of attention, but mostly in the way of unbalanced criticisms on both sides of the issue. So, what precisely does form entail?

Form entails structure. The structure of liturgy consists of specific components for the delivery of God's Gospel-gifts.

The simplest division of components in the structure of worship comes in the form of Word and Sacrament, or liturgy in the narrow sense. Here the most basic service of Word and Sacrament consists of these elements: Scripture readings, sermon, Creed, prayer of the church, words of institution, and distribution of the body and blood of Christ. On this level of form these structural elements, including the Sacrament of Holy Baptism, are non-negotiable. They are non-negotiable because they reflect the basic requirements for the unity and the orthodoxy of the church according to Article VII of the *Augsburg Confession.*

In addition to holding to this basic form of the church's liturgy, there is another issue—the issue of a liturgy that is externally familiar and easily recognizable to God's people. While this can only be played out in local contexts, it must be done with careful consideration for our collective identity as Lutherans, and the longer, historic view of our identity as Christians. Consequently, what I have just outlined according to the bare simplicity of liturgy in the narrow sense does not entirely resolve the issue.

Beyond this simplicity of form are the many other elements of the church's liturgy which have been added and developed over the centuries, for example, the Trinitarian invocation, the preparation or corporate confession and absolution, the *Introit*, the *Kyrie*, the hymn of praise or *Gloria in Excelsis*, the *Gloria Patri*, and all the rest down to the final benediction. Within this structure should be added the singing of psalms, hymns, and spiritual songs. All of these structural elements of liturgy are an aspect of form. This is what I have called liturgy in the broad sense. Although liturgy in the narrow sense is sufficient for delivery of the Gospel, liturgy in the broad sense further facilitates access to the Gospel. While liturgy in the narrow sense is non-negotiable, liturgy in the broad sense is negotiable.

In direct relation to the church's liturgy in the broad sense, form also entails style. The style of liturgy is more of an abstraction and is more difficult to define.

Style is really an issue of aesthetics, or the art of the form. We should certainly be concerned about the excellence of what we do. Poorly executed traditional form is no better than poorly executed contemporary form. We must always be diligent about presenting to the world the new creation of the Gospel. However, we also must not be slaves to the form, as it is not the form that effects our salvation, but the content of the form in the Gospel and the sacraments. This is a criticism that cuts in both directions. The Apostle Paul wrote to the Corinthians: "But we have this treasure in earthen vessels, that the excellency of the power may be of God, and not of us." (2 Corinthians 4:7; KJV)

There are clear stylistic differences between traditional and contemporary forms of worship. Regardless of whether the form is classical-traditional or contemporary, what is most important is edification in the Gospel for people of specific place, time, and circumstance as *Formula of Concord* X puts it, that is, the local congregation.

The third basic element of the church's liturgy is function. Now, no one can claim that these criteria define worship only in functional terms. This model describes function as only one aspect of the church's liturgy, alongside essence and form. According to the Lutheran Confessions the function of liturgy involves five specific things: delivery of the Gospel, decorum or good order in the church, catechesis (or teaching), edification in the Gospel, and the avoidance of frivolity and offense.

The primary function of liturgy is the delivery of the Gospel. The delivery of the Gospel works the forgiveness of sins. This takes place through the pure proclamation of the Gospel of the crucified and risen Savior and through the giving of the sacraments in accordance with the Word of God. This is arguably the most important function of liturgy and deserves our constant attention. Get the Gospel right and the rest follows. If we get the Gospel wrong, because we are using contemporary forms uncritically, then we put at risk the very salvation of the souls for whom Christ gave his life on the cross. If the lyrics of a contemporary worship song, or even a traditional hymn for that matter, function in such a way that they obscure or skew the delivery of the Gospel, then they are not appropriate for use in the service of God's house. The single most important function of liturgy is the delivery of the Gospel.

Function also involves decorum and good order in the church. In the context of giving instructions to the worshiping assembly at Corinth the Apostle Paul wrote: "For God is not a God of confusion but of peace." (1 Corinthians 14:33) And, "all things should be done decently and in order." (1 Corinthians 14:40) This is an aspect of liturgy which brings us to consider that in the Gospel and the sacraments we are the recipients of a divine mystery, before which every boast is silenced and every tongue is loosed in joyous praise.

Jesus may be our buddy. But he is also our Lord. Jesus is our friend. But he is also our King. Jesus certainly is our loving shepherd. But he is also the Creator and Sustainer of the universe, to whom alone every knee will bow and every tongue confess. Decorum and good order in the Christian assembly serve the proclamation of the Gospel in sermon, sacraments, and ceremonies. Good order leads the worshiping assembly from the cross to the resurrection, from confession to absolution, from our sinful depravity to the hope of new life in Christ.

Function further involves catechesis—teaching God's people the truth of the Gospel from the Trinitarian invocation to the benediction. The insatiable appetite for change and novelty in worship works against teaching God's people the truths of the Christian faith. Liturgical repetition assists the worshiping assembly in its reception of the Gospel-gifts and frees the people to engage in a more meaningful reflection on the substance being delivered there. Bland sermons with little or no application, hymns (and songs) that are unfamiliar to the congregation and difficult to sing, too many announcements during the execution of the liturgy. It's no wonder people are dissatisfied with worship. Spending the time it takes to prepare for the liturgy to be consistent and well-executed is an aspect of ministry that needs to be rediscovered.

Doing liturgy well, and doing it the same week after week, promotes liturgical catechesis and the reception of the Gospel through the liturgy. That does not mean, however, that innovation has no place in Lutheran worship. I am not here promoting arbitrary, weekly innovation, but a conscientious, well-thought-out liturgical expression that engages the hearts and the minds of God's people. Contemporary form need not necessarily be equated with shallow, weekly liturgical innovation, if we are conscientious about the catechetical function of liturgy.

Function of liturgy also involves the edification of the church. Here, localized cultural expressions will impact decisions regarding edification. Some contexts are rooted in liturgical chant, incense, and ornate vestments. Others are rooted in no frills and simpler expectations. Some forms are more elaborate; some are more basic. It is the historic confessional judgment of the church that such forms have absolutely nothing to do with the unity and orthodoxy of the church and that consciences must never be bound because of differences in forms of humanly instituted ceremonies in the church's liturgy.

Finally, the function of the church's liturgy includes the avoidance of frivolity and offense. In various congregations one can encounter heavy metal music, grunge music, clown worship, fireworks in worship, and parading animals up and down the aisles. These are among the most glaring instances of frivolity and offense. These are the kinds of things that distract the worshiper from receiving the Gospel.

All of this taken together is Lutheran theology for Lutheran worship, a model for worshiping as Lutherans—essence, form, and function—which may serve as criteria for critiquing worship forms before using them in the Lutheran congregation. **(See Appendix-2)** If a local congregation chooses to include "contemporary" forms in its worship, what is included must be carefully crafted according to what is given in the Gospel and according to the Scriptures. This is necessary, if it is to be a faithful expression of our Lutheran identity. The model for worshiping as Lutherans outlined here (essence, form, and function) may serve the church as a tool for critiquing worship songs and other worship materials, and for setting reasonable limits when including these forms.

SUMMARY POINTS

- The model for worshiping as Lutherans entails three things—essence, form, and function.

- The essence of worshiping as Lutherans is the Gospel, justification, the theology of the cross.

- The form of worship entails both structure and style.

- There are five functions of worshiping as Lutherans. They are: 1) delivery of the Gospel, 2) decorum and good order, 3) catechesis, 4) edification, and 5) the avoidance of frivolity and offense.

STUDY / DISCUSSION QUESTIONS

1. Why is it important that we hold to the principle: Lutheran theology for Lutheran worship? What happens when we do not do this?

2. Where do rites and ceremonies in worship come from?

3. What are the three basic elements of worshiping as Lutherans?

4. What is the essence of Lutheran worship? Why is it important to be aware of this?

5. Where is the distinction between traditional and contemporary forms of worship located in the model for worshiping as Lutherans? How does this help us understand the extent to which these are important (or not important) for our identity as Lutherans?

6. Why is it important to avoid frivolity and offense in our worship practices? How would you define frivolity and offense in today's context? Remember to craft your answer in such a way that you are being respectful to the person who might disagree with you.

9

Worship and Culture

WHAT DO you think of when you hear the word "culture"? Do you think of floats and marching bands in a parade? Maybe you think of classical music on an FM radio station, or attending the local symphony. Do you think of a wine and cheese party with friends, and your favorite music in the background? Or maybe you imagine rodeo events, roping steers, barrel races, and riding bulls. Or your definition of culture could be more focused on Rock & Roll or popular music, maybe even Folk Music or Bluegrass. Where I grew up as a child there was a local fall festival called the Apple Jubilee. There was a carnival, a parade, a beer garden, barbecued pig, cotton candy, and a lot of community. All of these things are different expressions of human culture.

In this last chapter I will focus the discussion on worship and culture. What is the relationship between worship and culture? Is worship transcendent of culture? Some have said this. How does the church address the difficult problem of remaining faithful to Christ and what he has given in the pure Gospel and the sacraments, and still fulfill its mission of proclaiming the Gospel to the world?

By suggesting that worship is "transcendent" of culture, some in the church have adopted a Platonizing ideal with the intention of countering the cultural depravity of the West. This is the kind of response we make when we have a model of confession that corrects an error by confessing the error's opposite. But we have already seen that this is not the Lutheran model of confession. I would argue that holding to the "transcendence" of worship as an act of confession against culture is tilting at windmills and unnecessarily divisive to the church.

The present state of cultural depravity is in part the result of a shift in the historic role the church has played in the formation of culture. Gone are the days when the church was the primary influence on the arts. While this was true during the Medieval Period, it has long since ceased to be the case. The degeneration of the church's normative role in relation to culture has led many to capitulate to culture. Christian values submerge beneath the anti-values of the culture. This capitulation on the part of some has led others to a reactionary posture of radical opposition to our culture, an opposition that attempts to turn liturgy into a counter-cultural, confessional response.

Much has been written in the last couple of decades about the relationship between the church and culture. Many of these studies, however, lay too heavy an emphasis on what is not right within our culture. While there is much that may be said about what is not right within the present culture, what we really must be working toward is a clearer understanding of the relationship between culture and worship. This must not just devolve into a mindless criticism of culture as an inadequate authority for shaping people's needs in worship. What we need is the honest, proactive recognition that our culture is no longer predominantly characterized by a classical aesthetic. In other words, because of the predominance of popular music virtually everywhere—in shopping malls, theaters, athletic events, concerts, restaurants, even schools—it seems that most people today have difficulty appreciating classical forms of music.

Although popular aesthetic is peculiar to neither the latter half of the twentieth century nor the beginning of the twenty-first century, the actual shift from the predominance of a classical to that of a popular aesthetic began in earnest in the 1920s, '30s and '40s with the advent of the radio culture (Jazz & Flapper music: Bye Bye Blackbird, Ha-Cha-Cha, Doin' the Raccoon, My Blue Heaven, Yes We Have No Bananas; Great White Way Orchestra, Al Jolson, George Gershwin, Jelly Roll Morton, Hoagy Carmichael, Cole Porter, Louis Armstrong, Dizzy Gillespie, Benny Goodman, Bing Crosby, Glenn Miller). The shift exploded in the 1950s, probably due to the already increasing popularity of television (Richie Valens, Frank Sinatra, Fats Domino, Little Richard, Chuck Berry, Big Bopper, Buddy Holly, Elvis Presley, Jerry Lee Lewis). The shift took a widely deviant turn with the popular acceptance of hedonism growing out of anti-authoritarian ideology in the 1960s (Eric Burdon & the Animals, the Beatles, the Rolling Stones, the Who, Carlos Santana, Blind Faith, Traffic, Cream; and psychedelic-acid rock: the Warlocks/the Grateful Dead, Big Brother & the Holding Company, Jimi Hendrix, It's A Beautiful Day, Quicksilver Messenger Service, Jefferson Airplane). And finally, if it had not done so already, the shift from the predominance of a classical to a popular aesthetic arguably reached the status of a paradigm shift by the 1970s (Led Zeppelin, Pink Floyd, Jethro Tull, Frank Zappa & the Mothers of Invention, Little Feat, Chicago, the Doobie Brothers, the Eagles, Queen, Steely Dan).

The anti-Vietnam War movement in the 1960s and early '70s and the general disappointment with the political establishment following the exposure and prosecution of the Watergate scandal in 1974 went a long way to fuel anti-authoritarian attitudes and ideology. Now, here we are, nearly four decades after the paradigm shift has occurred, still scratching our heads over what to think or do. Are we not capitulating to culture to the point where the church is no longer distinguishable from our secularized surroundings? Are we not repristinating ourselves into a corner out of fear, apprehension, and judgmentalism?

Two arguments run past each other. One is a historical construct that sees the church no longer as the force it once was for shaping culture. With the advent of the Renaissance, the Reformation, and the early modern period, the church only began to lose its influence on culture. The pace of this loss hastened with the development of scientific philosophy in the seventeenth century and the arrival of the Enlightenment and Rationalism in the eighteenth century—Renè Descartes, Baruch Spinoza, Voltaire, Immanuel Kant. Søren Kierkegaard's leap of faith, Friedrich Nietsche's nihilism, and Charles Darwin's *On the Origin of Species* with its introduction of evolutionary method as philosophical science, all shaped the intellectual landscape of the mid to late nineteenth century. The development of biblical criticism in the nineteenth and twentieth centuries has largely contributed to popular mistrust of the Bible, due to the groundbreaking critical work of scholars like Julius Wellhausen, Gerhard von Rad, and Rudolph Bultmann. And the onslaught of postmodernism in the philosophical work of Michel Foucault and Jacques Derrida have further eroded the world's perception of the church and its message, until we arrive at the veritable mess in which we find ourselves today. Those who advance this argument insist that, regardless of how we came to this state of affairs in the relationship between the church and culture, we must do something to bridge the gap. Sometimes this "something" goes well beyond what the church has historically or traditionally done.[1]

The other argument is also a historical construct, that Revivalism in American Protestantism during the eighteenth, nineteenth, and early twentieth centuries freely made use of music derived from popular cultural forms in order to attract people to its message. Consequently, when congregations attempt to make contact with the present-day popular culture by focusing on worship forms or music styles, we must view these attempts as extensions of nineteenth- and twentieth-century American Revivalism and all the pietistic theological baggage that goes with it. Yet this construct would render too narrowly the scope of the question, in order to confine the church's response to the problem.

Is worship truly transcendent of culture or has the church historically made the effort to use worship in such a way that the Gospel speaks to every culture's unique context? The Lutheran Confessions explicitly address changing times and circumstances as this relates to the local congregation's authority to change its worship forms. We appreciate the traditions created by the church in the past, with Gospel-openness to the creation of new forms in the church today.

The relationship between worship and culture is something that warrants careful consideration. If too much em-

---

1. In the interests of fully disclosing my own personal assumptions, this is the construct I find most convincing.

phasis is placed on cultural change, we run the risk of making culture our normative authority in our efforts to connect worship with people who happen to be involved (or even enamored!) with a particular culture. On the other hand, if the way we worship is over-emphasized and we make worship our normative authority over against culture on principle, then a paralysis occurs in the sense that the church ceases to understand the fullness of its missional role as the body of Christ in relation to the world. Historically the church has always understood liturgy in the context of culture.

The basilica was a Roman style of architecture that impacted both synagogue and church, and still does to this day. Both Semitic and Greek forms impacted the words of the early church's song as well as its theological discourse. Aramaic gave way to Greek. Greek gave way to Latin. And Latin for the last five hundred years has been giving way to the language of the people in local liturgical contexts.

In the fourth century an orthodox church father by the name of Ephrem of Syria used Gnostic hymn forms to convey the message of Christ's Gospel in orthodox theology. Harmonius, the son of the Gnostic Bardasanes, gained a popular following among large numbers of people because of the style of music he used for his hymns. Ephrem realized how the people were enamored with "the elegance of the diction and the rhythm of the melody," so he composed hymns in similar meters "in accordance with the doctrines of the church." Ephrem used the Gnostic forms of Harmonius to promote the true biblical teaching of Christ.

Likewise in the fourth century Basil of Caesarea, who wrote the earliest clear presentation of the biblical doctrine of the Trinity, was attacked by a group of pastors in Neocaesarea for certain worship practices in his congregation. They accused Basil of using an innovative style of music in the singing of psalms in worship. Basil responded by claiming that the Neocaesarean pastors were straining at a gnat while swallowing a camel, and that they were neglecting the most important law of Christ, the law of Christian love. The church has always understood liturgy in the context of culture.

We have already seen how the local congregation has the confessional authority and freedom to order its own rites and ceremonies in worship. But what would this actually look like in practice? God provides all congregations with the gifts he wants them to have. If your congregation has an organist, draw upon the talents of that organist to be used in the service of the church. What if there is no organist and God has provided you with a pianist instead? Use the gifts God gives. What if there is no pianist? Is there a guitarist in your midst? Invite that person, who is specially gifted by God, to share this gift in the service of the church. Does someone play a woodwind or a stringed instrument? Or maybe brass or percussion? In one of the congregations I served as pastor, we used a tuba for the Christmas Eve service. As bizarre as that may seem, it was one of the most beautiful expressions of music in service to the proclamation of God's grace in the birth of the Savior we had ever heard.

It is rare for one church to have so many different gifts. Most congregations are smaller and have only one or maybe just a few individuals with God-given musical abilities. Every congregation should use its own individual gifts as God has given them, for the edification of his people in that particular place.

Psalm 150 provides helpful guidance here. The psalm begins by exhorting the faithful to "Praise God in his sanctuary!" So the beginning premise of this psalm was the worship life of God's people in the Jerusalem temple. You may recall that in the Torah there were dozens of specifically prescribed forms for the liturgy of the priests and the people. (Leviticus) The sacrifices were prescribed in minute detail. The clothing of the priests was prescribed in minute detail (even down to the color and shape of their underwear!). The use of incense was prescribed in minute detail. There was a specific form or structure of worship that God in his wisdom prescribed for his people.

Psalm 150 also reveals that there was an element of freedom in the execution of the worship of God's people that went along with all the prescribed forms. "Praise him with trumpet sound; praise him with lute and harp! Praise him with tambourine and dance; praise him with strings and pipe! Praise him with sounding cymbals; praise him with loud clashing cymbals! Let everything that has breath praise the LORD! Praise the LORD!" Now, this is not just referring to the private devotion of God's people at home. This exhortation refers to the public worship of God's people in the Jerusalem temple!

How does the church relate cultural change to its worship forms today? We should be careful not to accommodate worship forms too narrowly to culture. The temptation to "market the church" is misguided. And we should be aware that the secular community is onto the hypocrisy of an American Evangelical Christianity which has no scruples about tailoring its message to appeal to the consumer appetites of Western materialism, to the extent that the church and American popular culture become virtually indistinguishable. Did you want a latte with that praise chorus? How about a scone or a cookie? People today want their church to be "real," not "relevant."

To move beyond what people "want," to what people "need" is what worshiping as Lutherans aims to do. As we have already seen, the fundamental need that is common to all human experience is the need for forgiveness in Christ, without any inner inclination to merit or worthiness whatsoever. If it is indeed grace, as the Scriptures teach, then it is all about Christ.

Sally Morgenthaler is a displaced Lutheran. At least that is what she calls herself, a displaced, out-of-the-box Lutheran who writes on trends in the emerging church movement.[2] In a book titled, *Exploring the Worship Spectrum*, Morgenthaler contributed an essay in which she criticizes our present-day culture, and describes the religious contours of postmodernity.[3] According to Morgenthaler, we postmoderns are fascinated with the supernatural and hungry for mystery. We thrive on diversity and crave community—"everything from antique gun clubs to eBay chat rooms."

There is one characteristic, however, that overshadows all our postmodern predilections, according to Morgenthaler, and that is our personal and societal brokenness. (It seems to me we used to call that sin.) Morgenthaler observes that the utopian dream of the scientific age is so far in the rear view mirror as to be only a vague, distant memory. What we have

2. From an interview with Morgenthaler titled "Sally Morgenthaler [author of 'Worship Evangelism'] discovers the underbelly of 'cutting edge' church," on the EMERGINGCHURCH.INFO website.

3. Sally Morgenthaler, "Emerging Worship," *Exploring the Worship Spectrum: 6 Views*, Paul A. Basden, ed. (Grand Rapids: Zondervan, 2004) 217–30.

instead is the sobering reality that we do not have control of our lives and we are faced with the painful reality of having to come to grips with our human limitations.

In response to Morgenthaler's observation I would simply ask, what will it take for us, the Lutheran Church, to wake up to the reality of desperate people all around us? We have a message of hope and salvation that does not conform to the latest trend, but speaks directly to the postmodern "brokenness" and "loss of control" Morgenthaler writes about. Sin has been, is, and always will be sin, whether you call it missing the mark, rebellion, imperfection, brokenness, or loss of control. The human condition is by nature alienated from God and is in profound need of the hope we have in the sweet, healing Gospel of salvation by God's grace in Jesus Christ. ". . . a broken and contrite heart, O God, you will not despise." (Psalm 51:17)

Morgenthaler argues that emerging churches in the early years of the twenty-first century have something to offer worship that contemporary worship of the 1980s and '90s has failed to live up to. She argues that contemporary worship is too "self-referencing—focused on human perceptions, needs, feelings, and desires," as she puts it. I whole-heartedly agree. Morgenthaler argues that emerging churches offer something better, a "realignment" as she calls it, which reinstates what she calls "Creator-referenced, God focused expressions."

While Morgenthaler's critique of contemporary worship is spot on, the solution the emerging church movement offers does not go far enough. I might concede that it is a step in the right direction, changing our focus from "felt-needs" to a God-centered worship, but it is only a small step. The emphasis is still too worshiper-focused. Emerging church worship focuses on these three central points: who God is, who the worshiper is in relation to God, and who the worshiper is created to become. Emerging worship may be focused more on God than the cliche contemporary worship of the 1980s and '90s, but it is still first-article (of the Creed), "Creator-referenced" worship. And if emerging worship is first-article centered, then ultimately there is nothing to distinguish it from the worship of any other religious tradition, be it Jewish, Muslim, or Hindu.

Lutherans who use contemporary worship today are, generally speaking, too soft in their theological discernment of the songs they sing (although a softened theological discernment is a problem for most Lutherans today, not just those who use contemporary worship). The answer is not just to avoid contemporary forms altogether. The answer is to harden our theological metal, and to stop rejecting out of hand the value of growing in our Christian faith and knowledge. Concrete must be "cured" (or hardened) before it is driven on. Discernment comes from having knowledge of the truth, and we have knowledge of the truth by reading and studying the Scriptures. A healthy body comes from exercising the body. A lack of exercise results in a soft body, and a host of other health problems. Why should we expect it to be any different when it comes to our faith and discerning right from wrong? (Hebrews 5:12–14)

Brian McLaren, who has been one of the most visible leaders of the emerging church movement, has said that the cross is not the center of the Christian faith. He refers to the cross as a distraction and false advertising for God—a "distraction" and "false advertising"(!).[4] While there is much that we can learn from this movement and what it means for people seeking a relationship with God in today's postmodern

4. McClaren's comments are recorded on The Bleeding Purple Podcast blogsite at http://bleedingpurplepodcast.blogspot.com.

culture, there are fundamental flaws of false doctrine running through the teachings of some leaders of this movement, not the least of which is the unsound deprecation of the cross, when it is the cross that should be at the center of the church's theology, and should always be at the center of our worship.

I hope that I have been absolutely clear about what the center of worshiping as Lutherans is. Lutheran Christian worship is Gospel-centered, not first-article "Creator-referenced," but second-article forgiveness-of-sin referenced. Lutheran Christian worship is focused on the cross and God's gracious act of love in giving his Son for us and for our salvation. This is genuine Christian worship that speaks to the real needs, the real brokenness, and the absolute desperate condition of having lost all control, the sin of human beings in every age and every culture and its absolutely devastating consequence—alienation from God.

The answer to the question, How does worship make contact with culture? cannot be sought in selling out the church, or conforming to the latest trend of disillusioned Americans groping about in their "emerging" search for meaning in relation to God. Worship makes meaningful contact with culture by remaining faithful to what our Lutheran tradition has consistently, through the centuries, held to be non-negotiable. What the church has consistently held to be non-negotiable are not humanly instituted ceremonies in worship, but what is given by God—the pure Gospel and the divinely instituted sacraments. These are the non-negotiables.

The non-negotiables then shape the church's worship in such a way that the Gospel is clearly proclaimed in any given culture. It is when the Gospel and the sacraments are given to the task of shaping worship, that worship is then faithful to engage culture with the real presence and the eternal hope of Jesus Christ. This is why we rejoice in the received liturgical traditions of the church with Gospel openness and gratitude, not with entrenched, reactionary, rigid, and pedantic liturgical repristination.

Gospel openness frees the church to use its worship as an intra-cultural expression of the Gospel. This is why I agree with Morgenthaler in part when she writes that pastors and worship leaders must become more intentional about choosing and writing contemporary music that has "musical and theological excellence." Those are her terms, not mine. I would say that we should be more intentional about choosing and composing contemporary music that is faithful to our theology of worship, keeping it centered on the Gospel of our incarnate, crucified, and risen Savior, Jesus Christ, and the precious gifts of the sacraments.

Liturgical form is malleable clay in the hands of God the Creator, molded and shaped according to his good pleasure. What is "transcendent" is the essence of the mystery of the Gospel revealed in Jesus Christ, as the Apostle Paul wrote: "If then you have been raised with Christ, seek the things that are above, where Christ is, seated at the right hand of God. Set your minds on things that are above, not on things that are on earth. For you have died, and your life is hidden with Christ in God." (Colossians 3:1–3) This is true biblical transcendence. What is concrete, on the other hand, earthy if you will, is the sound of the human voice, the melody of the music, the rhythm of the beat, the sight, smell, taste, and touch of the Triune God in the midst of his people delivering his Gospel-gifts in Word and Sacrament.

Historically speaking the church has always understood that there is an essence of worship that remains the same and that there are then all those things that revolve around the essence of worship. This outer orbit of worship consists of external forms that change in different cultures through time. But we must also be cautious in our approach to this "outer orbit" of worship. We must be careful that we not allow ourselves to be taken captive by any given culture. Such a capitulation to culture is nothing short of idolatry, and we all know in the end where idolatry leads.

While the essence of the Gospel mystery must be kept pure, the concrete expression of the form presents every Christian community with a unique challenge. That challenge is to make the mystery accessible in each community's peculiar cultural context and still maintain the integrity of the mystery. The question then becomes: Are we in the church prepared to face this challenge?

SUMMARY POINTS

- The church has always understood its liturgy in the context of culture.

- Worship is not "transcendent" of culture; it uses cultural forms to communicate the message of the Gospel in every local context.

- Biblical Christian worship is not first-article-of-the-Creed focused; that is, its primary purpose is not to help us understand what God has created us to be.

- Biblical Christian worship is second-article-of-the-Creed focused; that is, its primary purpose is to deliver forgiveness of sins from Christ to us.

STUDY / DISCUSSION QUESTIONS

1. Some today say that the church's worship should be totally distinct from present-day popular culture. Historically, how has the church viewed the relationship between worship and culture? Read 1 Peter 4:10–11. How might a biblical passage like this be applied to the worship-culture question today?

2. According to the "emerging church" point of view, what is the essence of worship? How does this compare to the Lutheran Christian point of view? What can we learn in a positive way from the emerging church point of view on worship? What should we be cautious of?

3. Consider Morgenthaler's criticisms of 1980s and '90s contemporary worship songs. Are her criticisms fair? If Morgenthaler is correct on this point, what might be a proper biblical response as Lutheran Christians?

4. Why is a softened ability to discern errors in some con-temporary worship songs (or even in some traditional hymns) a problem for worshiping as Lutherans? What is the proper, biblical solution to this problem?

5. According to the Lutheran point of view, what is the relationship between worship and culture?

Conclusion

F OR THE last hundred pages or so I have given you a small glimpse into a pastor's heart and mind, and I have shared with you my own experience with worship in the Lutheran congregation. One of the congregations I served chose to have a contemporary service. I did not impose this choice on them. In fact, it was just the opposite. They imposed it on me, but only after we carefully studied the Scriptures and the Lutheran Confessions together. This little book is the direct result of that study. Appendix-1 contains an outline for worshiping as Lutherans, one that is almost identical to the service my congregation adopted.

I hope that in these pages I have given you useful theological and practical tools to apply to your own worship context. We have explored together some of the points over which the church is troubled, and I have attempted to provide you with a workable solution that could bring together again those who have been divided by the "worship wars" on several levels. It is also my fervent hope that I have given you a basis for furthering the conversation with each other in a way that promotes the Gospel in Christ's church.

If we truly hope for this coming together to happen among Lutherans who have differing minds about worship, then we must all be willing to give something up. I cannot tell you what that something is. This is something that can only be determined in every local congregation in faith and love. Luther put it this way in his *German Mass*:

> But while the exercise of this freedom is up to everyone's conscience and must not be cramped or forbidden, nevertheless, we must make sure that freedom shall be and remain a servant of love and of our fellow-man. Where the people are perplexed and offended by these differences in liturgical usage, however, we are certainly bound to forego our freedom and seek, if possible, to better rather than to offend them by what we do or leave undone. Seeing then that this external order, while it cannot affect the conscience before God, may yet serve the neighbor, we should seek to be of one mind in Christian love.[1]

Only one year prior to this, in 1525, Luther wrote in his *Exhortation to the Livonians Concerning Public Worship and Concord*: "Now even though external rites and orders . . . add nothing to salvation, yet it is un-Christian to quarrel over such things and thereby to confuse the common people. We should consider the edification of the lay folk more important than our own ideas and opinions."[2] It warrants being stated again. Luther's warnings can be applied in both directions in today's conversation about worship.

If there are any specific points I want you to take away from your reading of this book, it would be these three: First, Lutheran theology for Lutheran worship. Christ and his cross are at the center. Lutheran theology of worship is built on, and grows out of, the theology of the cross—Christ crucified

---

1. *American Edition of Luther's Works*, 53.61.

2. Ibid., 53.47.

and risen from the dead for the forgiveness of all our sins. Lutheran theology of worship is the free delivery of God's unmerited grace and forgiveness of sins to God's people gathered by the Holy Spirit around the Word and the sacraments. Lutheran theology for Lutheran worship. Hold onto that.

Second, we distinguish what is given by God (liturgy in the narrow sense) from what is given by the church (liturgy in the broad sense). The distinctions that are inherent to liturgy—liturgy in the narrow sense and liturgy in the broad sense—the Gospel and the sacraments on the one hand, humanly instituted rites and ceremonies on the other—this distinction is crucial for addressing the issues the church faces today. We distinguish what is given by God from what is given by the church. Hold onto that.

Third, the Lutheran model of confession is to confess straight ahead the truth and freedom of the Gospel. It is not our model of confession to correct an error by confessing the error's opposite. When we do this, we only end up bending the sapling too far, as Martin Chemnitz put it, or we end up stumbling along in the ditch on the other side. The Lutheran model of confession is straightforward, unequivocal confession of the truth and freedom of the Gospel. Hold onto that.

These are the three things I hope you will take away from reading this book: first, Lutheran theology for Lutheran worship, that is, the theology of the cross; second, distinguishing clearly between liturgy in the narrow sense and liturgy in the broad sense, that is, distinguishing what is given by God from what is given by the church; and third, the Lutheran model of confession, unequivocal, straightforward confession of the truth and freedom of the Gospel.

Okay, there is a fourth thing. I want you to take away from this book that it is still possible to have a conversation about worship in the church. We can still talk to each other about worship. And when someone tries to enter the conversation in order to control it with anger, sarcasm, and name-calling, or to manipulate the conversation with wrong assumptions and bad methodology (again, a warning that cuts in both directions today), then call it for what it is. Remember, straightforward confession, and speak the truth in love, following the guidance of the Holy Spirit in his church through the pure Gospel and the sacraments administered in accordance with the divine Word. The brother or sister in Christ with whom we may disagree on *adiaphora*, but with whom we agree on the most important things (the Gospel and the sacraments), deserves to be treated with respect. When we honor each other by giving this respect, then it is still possible to have a conversation about worship in the church, even with those with whom we disagree on *adiaphora*.

The following is a quote from an article by Martin Franzmann titled, "Seven Theses on Reformation Hermeneutics." Franzmann wrote:

> The Word of God is an arrow with a perfect tip and a shaft without flaw, check, or blemish, feathered and balanced as no other arrow is; there is no arrow like it under the sun. The [Gospel] says: This perfect arrow is aimed at you; it will kill you, in order that you may live. The [Gospel] will not permit the church to become a Society for the Preservation of the Perfect Arrow.[3]

3. "Seven Theses on Reformation Hermeneutics," *CONCORDIA JOURNAL* 15.3 (July 1989): 337–50; see esp. 346–47.

To apply this to our conversation about worship, it would be prudent of us to heed Dr. Franzmann's admonition that we not allow ourselves to become "a Society for the Preservation of the Perfect Arrow." Dr. Franzmann was a great theologian and poet who composed hymns for the church, and we would do well to follow his example today by nurturing the poets and theologians of the church to write hymns and fresh components of liturgy, in both traditional and contemporary styles, that are faithful to the rule: Lutheran theology for Lutheran worship.

There is nothing wrong with taking risks with the created stuff God has given us, for shaping our external praise to him for his mercy and forgiveness in the crucified and risen Savior. In his *Latin Mass*, writing with regard to the usages of liturgy in the language of the people, Luther commented: "But poets are wanting among us, or not yet known, who could compose evangelical and spiritual songs, as Paul calls them [Col. 3:16], worthy to be used in the church of God."

I leave you with words of encouragement from Martin Chemnitz, from the end of his *Iudicium* on Adiaphora:

> But let us acknowledge our weaknesses and failures, let us seek forgiveness, and let us give thanks to God, who does not deal with us according to our iniquities, but with his unfathomable mercy for the sake of the glory of his name, and by the intercession of our Lord Jesus Christ he [corrects] our failures . . . . And let us pray for all who teach and learn by his Holy Spirit in the future, so that also . . . we may teach and learn in peace those things which are true and useful . . . in constant confession of the truth. To glorify God the Father of our Lord Jesus Christ is by his grace to preserve purity of doctrine and to pass it on to posterity. In this way concord

is brought about by the grace of God, useful to the
church and salutary to posterity.

SUMMARY POINTS

- Lutheran theology for Lutheran worship—the theology
  of the cross

- Distinguishing liturgy in the narrow sense from liturgy
  in the broad sense—what is given by God and what is
  given by the church

- The Lutheran model of confession—unequivocal,
  straightforward confession of the truth and freedom of
  the Gospel

- Welcome each other to the conversation in faith and
  love.

Appendix 1

An Outline for
Worshiping As Lutherans

WHAT WOULD an outline for worshiping as Lutherans, based on Scripture and the Lutheran Confessions, look like? Is it possible to create a Lutheran order of service in today's extraordinarily diverse context and still be faithful to the principle, Lutheran theology for Lutheran worship? Can we craft such an order of service, that would be recognizable to God's people on a wide scale while also allowing for freedom in the execution of the forms?

PREPARATORY RITE

Trinitarian Invocation
Confession of Sin & Absolution

WORD

Old Testament
Epistle
Gospel
Sermon
Nicene Creed
Tithes & Offerings
Prayer of the Church

SACRAMENT

Lord's Prayer
Words of Institution
Peace
Distribution
Blessing

Luther wrote in his *German Mass*, "We must arrive at a common standard to assess and control the profusion of orders." In many ways the problem today is similar to that of the sixteenth century: a profusion of orders without a common standard. By following the simple principle, "Lutheran theology for Lutheran worship," local congregations desiring to make use of contemporary forms can construct an order of worship that reflects our common desire to worship as Lutheran Christians in a recognizably Lutheran way.

Lutheran worship begins with a preparatory rite, that prepares the worshipers with a reminder of Holy Baptism. The Trinitarian invocation—"in the name of the Father and of the Son and of the Holy Spirit"—comes at the beginning of the service because it names the assembly with the name of the Triune God. This reminds the people of Holy Baptism by which God in his grace has placed his holy name on them and has adopted them into his family. This understanding of the Trinitarian invocation is sacramental with the pastor facing the congregation rather than the altar. The Trinitarian invocation communicates an environment of grace, by which God invites the worshipers to be restored to a right relationship with him. With this in view, the words "We make our beginning . . ." should not be added to the Trinitarian invocation, since they change the emphasis from God's gracious act in Baptism to our act of beginning the order of service.

As a preparatory rite, the confession and absolution, by proclaiming God's forgiveness, restores the worshipers to a right relationship with God. It highlights the reason Christians gather in the divine service. We human beings are sinful and we need the forgiveness God gives in Jesus Christ. Holy absolution delivers this forgiveness. Several different rites of confession and absolution could be prepared for sufficient variety. There are numerous examples of this in Scripture, from which a variety of rites may be crafted. Luther's comment, "What is changed according to God's Word is no innovation," is applicable here.[1] The practice of public confession and absolution should not be pitted against the salutary practice of private confession and absolution. To have such a relationship of trust with your pastor, or another Christian, is a great treasure and should be valued, rather than simply dismissed. The Trinitarian invocation and the confession and absolution have prepared the worshiping assembly for what follows. Historically, the church has maintained the order of its service in the gathering of God's people around the twofold gift of Word and Sacrament.

The Apostle Paul admonished Pastor Timothy: ". . . devote yourself to the public reading of scripture . . . ." (1 Timothy 4:13) Since the earliest times of the church, "the public reading of scripture" has been a practice of God's people gathered together by the Holy Spirit for the church's liturgy. Whether versicles and responses are used in connection with the readings should be left free. A brief explanatory note may or may

1. Quoted from Luther's "Exhortation to All Clergy Assembled at Augsburg," *American Edition of Luther's Works*, 34.39.

not be added before each reading, to assist the hearer in assimilating the meaning of the text as it is being read. To read the texts without interpretive comment may also be beneficial, depending on the context.

Proclamation of the Word in some form is a crucial component of divine service. This has very early attestation, going back at least to the practice of the synagogue (Luke 4:14–30). The proclamation of the Word, whether in the form of a sermon or a drama or some combination of the two, helps the worshiping community understand the biblical texts and apply them to their lives.

The Nicene Creed and the Apostles' Creed should not be allowed to fall into disuse in the church. We use the creeds because they are the church's historic confession of the pure Gospel. The Creeds are recognizable to the church for their purity, their clarity, and their simplicity in proclaiming the truth of the Gospel.

Tithes and offerings are an important part of the Christian life. The psalmist sings: "bring an offering and come into his courts!" (Psalm 96:8) The offerings of the church may be received here or some other suitable place in the order, or the opportunity may be provided upon entering or exiting the church.

Prayer is of the essence of what the church is and what the church does. The church prays to praise our Creator and Redeemer. And the church prays to make intercession for itself and for others. We praise God for his wisdom in creating the universe, and for his mercy and goodness in redeeming fallen man. We pray for civil rulers and for peace, so that the Gospel may be proclaimed freely. We make intercessions on behalf of the church, that our gracious God would bless her mission and her ministry. We pray for all enemies of the cross, that the Lord would turn their hearts with the kindness of his grace. We intercede for those who suffer, and those who grieve, that the Holy Spirit would grant healing, comfort, and the hope of the resurrection. And we pray for the servants of the church. For pastors and missionaries, for teachers and administrators, that the God of truth would make us faithful to teach and proclaim the truth and freedom of his Gospel.

The culmination of the gathering of God's people for Word and Sacrament is realized in the mystery of the Lord's Supper. By this Meal the crucified and risen Lord gives to his church his true body and blood for the forgiveness of sins, to strengthen faith and to comfort consciences burdened by sin. In this Meal he also gives the church a visible expression of its unity (1 Corinthians 10:15–17) and an open proclamation of the Gospel to the world. (1 Corinthians 11:26)

The Lord's Prayer has historically been connected to the celebration of the Lord's Supper. The use of this prayer has very early attestation in the church. Use it with joy, for the building up of the body of Christ.

The Words of Institution are essential to the church's worship. The Words of Institution should be spoken as they are given in Scripture (1 Corinthians 11:23–25); they should not be modified to give the appearance of spontaneity. Speak them clearly and loudly, so that the people will hear with certainty the precious Good News of the Gospel, that Christ's true body and blood, given and shed on the cross for the forgiveness of sins, is here for them.

It would be good, as far as possible, to restore the peace to its original character of reconciliation. While this may not be possible in terms of actual historic practice, the peace may be done in such a way that it encourages the people to live this reconciliation in the church and in their daily lives in the world. Like the confession of sins the peace could also take on a number of forms to emphasize in the hearts and minds of the people the depth and the breadth of Scripture's teaching on reconciliation. The peace may take its form from the theme of the day's sermon, demonstrating two things: the unity of the structure of Word and Sacrament, and whether the pastor's sermons have their primary emphasis in the Law or the Gospel. Clearly the peace, as genuine Christian reconciliation, grows and flourishes in the soil of the Gospel.

The distribution of the Sacrament may take place with the congregation kneeling, standing, or in continuous procession. It may be given by the pastor into the hand or into the mouth. All of this should be left free without binding consciences, taking into consideration the historic practice and culture of the local congregation. Consideration should be given for the one who distributes the body of the Lord. This is a point at which pastoral care is being exercised publicly, on behalf of and for the sake of the local congregation. If a non-ordained person or some other visiting ordained clergy not regularly called by the congregation assists in the distribution, then it is most appropriate according to 1 Corinthians 11:27–32 and *Augsburg Confession* Article XIV that the pastor of the local parish administer the body of Christ, in keeping with his responsibility to give or to withhold the Sacrament. This responsibility should not be expected of another.

When dismissing those who commune with the words, "Go in peace," it is an unfortunate confusion of Law and Gospel to add the words, ". . . and serve the Lord." Why not rather include the words, ". . . Your sins are forgiven"? After all, in this Sacrament we have God's gracious act of forgiveness. Highlight this profound gift of God in the Sacrament, rather than lay the burden of the Law on the worshipers as they depart from the Lord's Supper.

The final blessing of the congregation may take the form of the Aaronic benediction from Numbers 6:22–27, the apostolic blessing from 2 Corinthians 13:14, or some other form suitable to the Christian assembly. Again, let the people leave the worshiping assembly with a blessing in the way of the Gospel, rather than an added exhortation to perform one's Christian duties, which runs in the way of the Law. When we add the words "serve the Lord" to the blessing, "Go in peace," this lays the burden of the Law on the worshiping assembly. Why not rather add the words, "You are free"? Let the sweet freedom of the Gospel have its way with God's people, and then see what the Holy Spirit will do in his church.

This structure is faithful to the purity of the Gospel and the right administration of the sacraments required for worshiping as Lutheran Christians. It is faithful to the historic pattern of the church's worship in Word and Sacrament. It retains enough of historic liturgical tradition that it is recognizable to any Lutheran traveling away from home. And it clearly communicates to God's people the truth and freedom of the Gospel.

It should also be noted that the order outlined here omits all the canticles and versicles, responses and chants inherent to traditional forms—the *Introit*, the *Kyrie*, the *Gloria in Excelsis*, the *Collect* of the day, the versicles and responses related to the Scripture readings, the Gradual, the Offertory, the Preface, the *Sanctus*, the *Agnus Dei*, the *Nunc Dimittis*, and the *Benedicamus*—all of these are omitted in this outline for worshiping as Lutherans. This is precisely what Luther did with his *German Mass*. Local congregations should be free to use or not use any of these historic elements of the church's worship, without being condemned by others for having more or fewer humanly instituted rites and ceremonies.

Baptism is included in this order when there is the opportunity for including an individual in the community of God according to the words and institution of Christ. Baptism with water "in the name of the Father and of the Son and of the Holy Spirit" is essential, without changing the words or the institution as these were given by Christ in Matthew 28:16–20.

The use of psalms, hymns, and spiritual songs may be interspersed throughout the service. This should be done with theological discretion and careful attention to the aesthetic flow or movement of the entire service.

A caveat regarding the flow and the movement of the entire service. Too many announcements or directions interspersed in and among the elements of the service are a distraction, rather than an aid, to the worshiper. If the congregation prints the service folder, then spoken directions are redundant (as well as annoying!). Instead of facilitating worship, they hinder the flow of worship. If the congregation prints its service folder and directions are still necessary, then whoever is responsible for the worship of the congregation needs to reevaluate the format of the bulletin. It may even be the case that the order itself needs to be reevaluated. Prepare a printed worship folder that simplifies rather than distracts the worshiper from receiving the Gospel. There is a simple rule to follow here: Minimize (or eliminate altogether) announcements and directions during the service proper. Give directions before the service (in the rare instance when a correction is necessary), and make announcements either before or after the service (preferably before).

This entire outline for worshiping as Lutheran Christians, presented in this appendix, is very similar to other Lutheran church orders prepared in the sixteenth and seventeenth centuries. It also follows Luther's theological basis for creating the *German Mass*. Lutheran theology for Lutheran worship.

Appendix 2

A Tool to Evaluate Songs for Worshiping As Lutherans

THE FOLLOWING is offered as a tool to help those who lead worship, and who desire to include contemporary forms in their worship. This tool may be used to evaluate songs for use in the Lutheran congregation. We may naively wish that such tools never be used in the church. But until Christ returns at the end of all things, to take the church to be his bride in heaven, there will continue to be hymns and contemporary songs that do not reflect the pure Gospel or the sacraments as they are given in God's Word. Hence the need for the church to use such tools as this.

This tool may be copied and used by pastors, worship leaders, worship committees, and anyone involved in preparing the church's worship. Use it not in a legalistic, criticizing, or controlling way, but in a spirit of rejoicing in the gifts God has given to his church, the purity of the Gospel and the sacraments given according to God's Word—in a spirit that guards the good deposit our loving God has entrusted to his redeemed and forgiven people (2 Timothy 1:14), but also in a spirit that hopes to share this precious good news of salvation with all people.

Name of Hymn/Song

Source of Hymn/Song (Hymnal or Songbook, etc.)

Suitable for faithful use: ____ Yes   ____ No

Comments:

1. What is the primary focus of the hymn/song? In other words, what is its **ESSENCE**? What does the hymn/song primarily refer to?

    ____ Justification (Gospel)   It is: ____ Christ centered
    what God has done
    for us in Christ   ____ Man-centered
    ____ Sanctification (works of faith)
    ____ Both Justification and Sanctification
    ____ Other . . .

2. Is the Gospel clearly stated? If not, why not?

    ____ Yes   ____ No

3. Is there a confusion of Law and Gospel? (E.g., "All you have to do is ask Jesus into your heart . . . .") If so, describe how Law and Gospel are confused.

    ____ Yes   ____ No

4. How are the sacraments (Baptism & the Lord's Supper) treated in this hymn/song?

    ____ Not at all
    ____ As God's work of grace
            (Baptism/correct emphasis)
    ____ As a good work we do or decision we make
            (Baptism/incorrect emphasis)
    ____ As body & blood of Christ
            (Lord's Supper/correct emphasis)
    ____ As symbols of body & blood
            (Lord's Supper/incorrect emphasis)

5. How would you classify this particular hymn/song? What is its **FORM**?

____ Traditional-Classical	____ Folk
____ Spiritual	____ Jazz
____ Contemporary	____ Soft Rock
____ Hard Rock	____ Other:

6. What is the **FUNCTION** of the hymn/song? (Check as many as you think characterize the hymn/song. More than one may apply.)

____ To Proclaim the Gospel to the World

____ To Encourage

____ To Teach the Gospel

____ To Edify

____ To Praise God

____ To Tell a Biblical Story

____ To Comfort Consciences Burdened by Sin

Others: ____

          ____

7. Does the hymn/song promote good order and decorum? In other words, does the hymn/song draw the worshiper to focus clearly on the Gospel, and not just on the style of the music? If there is frivolity or offense, explain why.

____ Yes, it promotes good order & decorum

____ No, it contains …

          ____ Frivolity   ____ Offense

Why? …

8. Is there anything you would change about the hymn/song?

____ Its Wording

____ Its Music / difficult to sing / distracts
          from the Gospel

____ Its Length / too long or too short

____ No Change

Glossary

Adiaphora—in ancient literature a Greek word describing an undifferentiated middle ground (the proverbial "gray area") of moral philosophy; during the Reformation the reformers used it to refer to humanly instituted ceremonies in worship that are neither commanded nor forbidden by God.

Confession—a word that has two very different, but equally important meanings. The first meaning is the most familiar: to confess one's sins. The second meaning is less familiar: to make a declarative statement of what one believes; the Creed, for example.

Cultus—a Latin word meaning "worship"; the sixteenth-century reformers often used this word when they referred to liturgy in the broad sense.

Gemeine—a German word the reformers used to refer to the local congregation, which they considered to have the confessional authority and freedom to order its own rites and ceremonies in worship.

Gospel—the good news that, because He loves us, God gave His Son Jesus Christ to die on the cross for us and to rise from the dead, to save humankind from sin and to give us the promise of eternal life.

Justification—God's gracious act of declaring the sinner righteous, that is, to be in a state of having been restored to a right relationship with God, because of what Jesus did on the cross.

Leitourgia—(pronounced "lay-tour-gee-a") the Greek word for liturgy.

Leitourgia divina adiaphora non est—a Latin slogan used by some who hold the point of view known as Liturgical Theology. The phrase means "the divine liturgy is not adiaphora."

Liturgical Theology—a school of thought, originating in the late nineteenth century from Eastern Orthodoxy and Roman Catholicism, that holds liturgy to be an authoritative standard above Scripture and all other theology in the church.

Liturgy—a synonym of worship.

Liturgy in the Broad Sense—all the humanly instituted rites and ceremonies in liturgy. This is worship that is not given by God. It is given by the church.

Liturgy in the Narrow Sense—the purity of the Gospel and the sacraments given in accordance with God's Word. This is the part of worship that is given by God.

Mass—a word used in the medieval church to refer to the church's worship as a sacrifice offered to God; during the Reformation the reformers used this word to refer to the church's worship (but not as a sacrifice in the medieval sense), and often they used it with special reference to the Lord's Supper.

Norm—an authoritative standard by which we measure or evaluate other things. In the Lutheran Church the only "authoritative standards," by which we measure or evaluate all teachings, are Scripture and the Lutheran Confessions in the *Book of Concord*.

Proof-texting—a method of reading texts by which we isolate passages and read them out of their contexts, in order to support our prior assumptions, rather than letting the hard data of the authoritative texts shape our assumptions and our understanding.

Repristination—the process of restoring old things to present use, always striving for the "pristine," or purest, form.

Sacraments—Holy Baptism, Lord's Supper.

Septuagint—the Greek translation of the Old Testament, which was originally written in Hebrew and Aramaic.